DEUTERONOMY

The Gospel of Love

DEUTERONOMY

The Gospel of Love

by

SAMUEL J. SCHULTZ

MOODY PRESS

CHICAGO

© 1971 by
THE MOODY BIBLE INSTITUTE
OF CHICAGO

0-8024-2005-2

Library of Congress Catalog Card Number: 72-155693

Printed in the United States of America

CONTENTS

PREFACE

DOES THE PENTATEUCH SUGGEST to you primarily the idea of law? Do you think of Moses as the lawgiver in contrast to Jesus as the one offering love and grace? Is the God of the Old Testament a God of war, judgment, and wrath, and the God whom Jesus revealed the Father of mercy and the God of love? If so, the following pages offer you some thought-provoking considerations.

The book of Deuteronomy is the most important book in the Old Testament from the standpoint of God's revelation to man. For years in his teaching of Old Testament survey, the author made only brief references to Deuteronomy as a book which merely reviews or repeats what precedes in the Pentateuch. Such, however, is not the case. It is one of the books most frequently cited and referred to in the New Testament (nearly two hundred times, according to the Greek New Testament edited by Aland, Black, Metzger, and Wikgren).

Deuteronomy represents the core of what God revealed to Moses at Mount Horeb. From the knowledge of his own experience and the failures of one generation of Israelites who had literally been redeemed from Egyptian bondage, Moses here summarizes, with a life-and-death perspective for the new generation, that which is significant and crucial to their welfare.

The word *love* is at the heart of the message. Neither a list of dos and don'ts, nor law, nor legalism, nor rules for living, nor good works, nor even a high moral standard was primarily in focus. Basic to all of these was a vital relationship with God—a relationship of love. Out of this love relationship issued all other considerations that were important to man.

Love for man was initiated by God and did not come in response to human action or activity. Although God's tender care had been bestowed upon all mankind, God's love for Israel began with His choice of Abraham, Isaac, and Jacob. God's love was manifested to the entire nation through their miraculous deliverance from Egypt.

As a recipient of God's love, which was evident in His redemption and constant care, the Israelite was expected to respond with wholehearted love and devotion. This response tapped all the resources of his entire being—heart, soul, mind, and strength. This love and devotion was exclusive. No other gods could be allowed or tolerated in such a relationship.

Out of this unique relationship with his God, the Israelite was to express his love horizontally to his neighbor. Only as he experienced being loved by God was he qualified to extend love to his neighbor. A keen realization of God's love provided the wellspring that enabled the Israelite to love his fellowman in the true sense.

It is this vertical and horizontal love relationship that Jesus pinpointed as the essence of all that God required of man to obtain eternal salvation (cf. Mt 22:35-40; Mk 12:28-34; Lk 10:25-28). The expert in the Mosaic law representing the Pharisees concurred with Jesus that the law of love was more important than all other considerations.

It was in the book of Deuteronomy that Jesus and the

religious leaders found the core of God's revelation to man in written form. Jesus also pointed out that this represented the essence of all that is written in the law and the prophets (the Old Testament). Consequently, we do well to study this book which provides us insight and understanding of the context in which this divine concept of love was revealed through and stated by Moses.

INTRODUCTION

Authorship

In current scholarship two basic viewpoints prevail concerning the authorship of Deuteronomy. According to some scholars this book was written during the seventh century B.C.; many others recognize Moses as the author, thus placing it much earlier.

A Late Composition

As early as 1805 a German scholar by the name of De Wette proposed the theory that the book of Deuteronomy was written shortly before the time of Josiah and used as the law-book for religious reforms. Wellhausen gave classic expression to this idea by proposing that a prophet compiled Deuteronomy 12-26 about 630 B.C. with the intention of centralizing worship in Jerusalem. According to this theory this book was deposited in the temple and then discovered by Hilkiah the high priest.[1]

The book of Deuteronomy in part, if not the whole, was identified as the "D" document. About 200 B.C. this document was combined with two narrative documents known as "J" and "E" (dated respectively about 950-850 and 750 B.C.) and the priestly document known as "P" (dated about 450 B.C.) to form the present Pentateuch. From the standpoint of literary partition, J was so designated because of its use of the divine name of "Yahweh" ("Jahveh" in

German) for God, whereas E was identified by the use of
the term *Elohim*. The D document was hortatory, and the
P document was primarily concerned with worship.

The J document, according to this theory, was written
in the wake of the great Hebrew kingdom that flourished
in the Solomonic era. Geographically it was associated
with Judah, which continued to be dominated by the
Davidic dynasty after the secession of the Northern tribes
in 931 B.C. The E document emerged as written literature
during the peak of economic and political prosperity in
the reign of Jeroboam II about 800-750 B.C. Recently
scholars favor the tenth century as the preferable date for
the J and E documents, J being written shortly before the
death of Solomon and E at the beginning of the Northern
Kingdom.

This theory has been modified so that Deuteronomic
traditions began with the sacred and cultic festivals during
the premonarchical era and were adapted and modified
later by the prophetic circles. The basic book of Deuteronomy was written during the seventh century when
Manasseh ruled in Jerusalem, and was completed after 586
B.C. when it became the introduction to the Deuteronomy-
2 Kings corpus of Israelite history. Subsequently it was
expanded editorially when it was added to the Genesis-
Numbers corpus to form the Pentateuch. Moses had nothing to do with what is reported in Deuteronomy, nor did
he have any part in the literary composition of the book.[2]

MOSES AS AUTHOR

Modern scholars such as E. J. Young, Gleason L.
Archer, and R. K. Harrison, who recognize the Old Testament in its unreconstructed form as a reliable and trustworthy record, hold with the older Christian and Jewish
tradition that the book of Deuteronomy offers an accurate

record of Moses' addresses to the Israelites on the Plains of Moab. Although he may have had scribes writing for him who may have provided geographical explanations and the account of his death, Moses was essentially responsible for its writing, so that he is the author of this book as well as the rest of the Pentateuch.

Internal claims within Deuteronomy indicate that these speeches were delivered orally in the last month of the forty-year period of Moses' leadership (1:3) and preserved in written copies (31:9, 24; cf. 31:24-26).

The law of Moses is repeatedly referred to in the historical records of Israel (Jos 1:7-8; 8:31-34; 23:6; Judg 3:4; 1 Ki 2:3; 11:33; 2 Ki 14:6; 21:8; Ezra 6:18; Neh 13:1). The prophets in their messages likewise reflect a knowledge of the law given through Moses. Is 1:10; 2:3; 5:24; 8:16, 20; Ho 4:6; 8:1, 12; Amos 2:4; Mic 4:2; Zep 3:4; and others).

Jesus, in His teaching, and the apostles pointed to Moses as the author of Deuteronomy as well as the Pentateuch (cf. Mt 19:8; Jn 5:46-47; 7:19; Ac 3:22; and Ro 10:5). For those who regard the Bible as a trustworthy and reliable book, it is difficult to disassociate Moses in the historical sense from personal involvement in the events as well as the writing of Deuteronomy.[3]

TITLE

The Jewish name for this book, *devarim* ("words"), is derived from the initial sentence in 1:1, "These are the words which Moses spake." Most unfortunate is the English title *Deuteronomy,* which is based on the Greek mistranslation of the phrase "a copy of this law" (17:18) as "this second law." Frequently this has conveyed the misleading interpretation that Deuteronomy merely represents a restatement of the Mosaic revelation. In Old Testament studies, the book of Deuteronomy is frequently considered a repetition of what preceded, and thus it is neglected for serious study and analysis.

"These are the words" (Heb., *devarim*) provides the clue to a proper interpretation of the book of Deuteronomy. Since Moses combines his farewell address with Israel's renewal of the covenant, these introductory words seem to indicate that Deuteronomy in its literary form is similar to treaties used during the second millennium B.C. expressing in written form the agreement between a suzerain, or sovereign ruler, and his vassal. Compared with this contemporary usage of the Mosaic times it seems reasonable to consider the text of Deuteronomy as providing in written form the renewal of the covenant relationship established between God (as sovereign) and the Israelites with Moses (the mediator).[4]

SUMMARY

The essence of the divine revelation given through Moses during the period of his leadership of the nation Israel is summarized in the book of Deuteronomy. Whereas Exodus, Leviticus, and Numbers relate the events and provide detail concerning the religion of Israel, Deuteronomy represents an emphasis upon that which is basically important for the Israelites in their relationship with God.

The books of Exodus, Leviticus, and Numbers form the necessary background for Moses' summary in Deuteronomy. Historically, Israel's redemption from Egyptian bondage, accomplished through Moses under divine guidance as narrated in Exodus 1-19, is essential to Moses' appeal to the new generation on the Plains of Moab. The matters concerning religion as revealed at Mount Sinai (Ex 20—Num 10), provided instructions for the Israelites in establishing a place of worship, guidance for worshiping

God through their offerings and festal seasons, and organizational details essential for the Israelites in order to live as God's chosen people while en route to Canaan. Although the account of Israel's journey from Mount Sinai to the Plains of Moab is brief (Num 10:11—22:1), it provides the basic facts concerning Israel's failure, which precipitated God's judgment of thirty-eight years of wilderness wanderings, during which an entire generation perished. This provided the essential background for understanding Moses' appeal to the generation which was facing the prospects of entering the land of Canaan.

The conquest and occupation of the territory east of Jordan was part of the experience of this new generation under Moses (Num 22-36). This success should have provided a reasonable basis for them to listen to Moses' appraisal of the past and the future as he turned the leadership over to Joshua.

The book of Genesis offers the introduction to the Mosaic revelation that is unfolded in the rest of the Pentateuch. God's relationship established with the Israelites under Moses was a continuation of the divine promises made to the patriarchs. God identified Himself to Moses as the God of Abraham, Isaac, and Jacob. The mighty acts of God manifested in redeeming Israel out of Egyptian bondage represented the fulfillment of the promises made to their forefathers. In this way, Genesis 12-50 provides the background for God's revelation through Moses.

Genesis 1-11 is essential for a proper understanding of the divine revelation to the patriarchs. After the divine punishment that came upon all mankind through the flood, Abraham was singled out as the father of a nation through whom all the nations of the world would be blessed. These chapters account for the beginning of all things as well as man, and trace man's history to the time of Abraham.

Against this background, the appeal Moses made orally to the Israelites becomes vitally significant. From a lifelong experience and a forty-year responsibility as leader of Israel, Moses addresses the new generation. Being keenly aware of the fact that the preceding generation had failed, Moses expresses concern that those who now faced the prospect of conquest and occupation should profit from the failures of the past. Beginning with the establishment of the covenant relationship at Mount Sinai, Moses highlights the experiences where their fathers disobeyed and refused to exercise faith in God (Deu 1-4).

Moses points out positively that the essence of Israel's relationship with God is one of mutual love. This is the basic commandment, and out of this relationship toward God issues the second commandment, which is to extend love toward others. This theme with its corollary is developed in Deuteronomy 5-11.

In chapters 12-26 the basic obligations of a God-related people are repeated and developed. With the changes of environment from wilderness conditions to permanent residence in Palestine, these covenant obligations are adapted and adjusted.

The alternatives for God-related people are clearly delineated by the prophet Moses in chapters 27-30. Blessings and extended mercies from God await those who reflect the fear of God in daily life. On the other hand those who became lax in their relationship with God and turn to other gods will be subjected to exile and curse. The people are challenged to continue in the commitment of wholehearted love for God.

Finally Moses makes arrangements for the continuity of this relationship between God and Israel, chapters 31-33. Joshua is appointed as his successor. Moses publicly expresses his blessings and benediction upon the people to whom he has made known what God had revealed to him.

In brief outline form, the book of Deuteronomy may be considered under the following main divisions.

DEUTERONOMY FOR TODAY

When Jesus pointed to the two basic essentials which represented the sum and substance of the Old Testament, He spoke of wholehearted love for God and of love for one's neighbor. These two commandments represent the core of the Mosaic revelation as delineated in Deuteronomy.

Much can be learned from the instructions given by Moses in this summary. The Israelites were carefully taught by Moses how to express their love for God and fellowmen in daily life. The fulfillment of the law of love according to Jesus brought with it the promise of eternal life (Lk 10:25-28). Although Jesus Himself came to exemplify the perfect fulfillment of the law of love, the Deuteronomic instructions are of great practical value for today's Christian who is concerned about expressing his love for God and for his fellowmen.

God has not changed nor has human nature since Mosaic times. The basic principles governing the relationship between man and God and between man and man are the same today as they were in Bible times. Cultural differences have occurred, but the basic principles are unchanged. The instructions peculiar to Deuteronomic times or the New Testament era must be adapted to the cultural situations in which we live today. The implementation of the law of love in daily life is as significant for us today as it was for the Israelites in Old Testament times and the disciples of Christ in the Christian era.

When we recognize that the Deuteronomic revelation provides the basis for the messages of the prophets, and that Jesus came to fulfill and complete God's revelation to mankind, then the book of Deuteronomy becomes crucially significant. Moses was the prophet par excellence in the Old Testament. Jesus was the greater prophet of whom Moses spoke (Deu 18:15-19, cf. Jn 1:21; 6:14; 7:40). A careful consideration of Deuteronomy provides today's God-fearing people with a better insight and understanding of life in its relationship to God and fellowmen.

Moses constantly appealed to the Israelites on the basis that God's grace and love had been bestowed upon them. This had been evident in their lives when God through His mighty acts redeemed them out of Egypt. The New Testament appeal is basically the same, in that the Christian acknowledges God's love and grace as it is manifested in Christ. This is evident in Christ's mighty power in providing redemption from the bondage of sin. God's grace and love were manifested in the Israelite culture through Moses in ancient times and fulfilled in Jesus Christ in New Testament times. The Israelite, who responded to God's revelation in Old Testament times with a wholehearted love, and the Christian, who responds to the New Testament revelation of Jesus Christ with a wholehearted commitment, can both be identified as God-fearing persons. Both share in the hope of eternal life. Consequently the parallel of the modern Christian with the Israelite under Moses and the disciples under Christ offers an enriching study for more effective living in terms of what God expects.

Note how often Moses admonishes his hearers "to remember" and "do not forget" (cf. 5:15; 7:18; 8:2; and other references). The realization of what God had done for them brought into focus the ethical characteristics of God, so that in turn the redeemed Israelite would practice humanitarian principles toward the less fortunate — the alien, the orphan, and the widow (10:18).

Over thirty times Moses tells the Israelites to "go in and possess the land which the Lord your God gives you." This offers a practical consideration in their relationship with God. They must do their part in taking possession and at the same time recognize that God is giving them the land to possess. God's provision through His grace and man's enterprise are both essential in man's attainments here on earth.

OUTLINE

The Transition—Moses to Joshua, 31:1—34:12

1

LESSONS FROM HISTORY

(1:1—4:49)

INTRODUCTION (1:1-5)

MOSES IS SPECIFICALLY IDENTIFIED as the speaker in the opening words of the book of Deuteronomy. The geographical location is the land of Moab, east of the river Jordan. The date for this address by Moses is the eleventh month of the fortieth year after the exodus.

The location is significantly important. The Israelites are on the verge of entering the land of promise. They are encamped on the Plains of Moab on the eastern edge of the Jordan valley, northeast of the Dead Sea. This location is designated as "beyond the Jordan" which is better translated as "Transjordan." Since such phrases are used six times in Deuteronomy (1:1, 5; 4:41, 46, 47, 49) to refer to the east side of the river and three times (3:20, 25; 11:30) to the west side it seems to have no bearing on the location of the author of Deuteronomy. Whereas the Israelites had long before reached a point of entrance after an eleven-day journey from Horeb, now nearly forty years later they are once more poised for occupying the promised land. This long period of wilderness wandering had a vital bearing on what Moses said to the Israelites anticipating the occupation of Canaan.

In retrospect, the focal point is Horeb and not the land of Egypt. It was at Horeb that the covenant between Israel and God was established. What had transpired since this relationship between Israel and God had been ratified at Mount Sinai was vitally important. It was this period of time, when Israel should have been experiencing the benefits of this relationship, that Moses examined in depth as he addressed the Israelites. Significant also is the fact that under Moses' leadership they already had defeated Sihon and Og, the two Amorite kings east of Jordan, and occupied their territory.

Moses was the speaker. It was Moses who was the mediator through whom God made His great revelation to Israel. Through Moses' leadership the mighty acts of God had been manifested in releasing the Israelites from the clutches of Egyptian enslavers (Ex 1-19). Through Moses were given the tablets of stone which were engraved with the terms of the covenant, the instructions for building the tabernacle as a worship center, the organization of the priesthood and levitical service, the instructions for bringing their sacrifices, and guidance for observing the feasts and seasons, and the organization of the camp of Israel (Ex 20-40, Lev 1-27; Num 1-10). It was Moses who had led them on the eleven-day journey in anticipation of entering the promised land. It was Moses who patiently provided leadership during the thirty-eight years of wandering and marking time while the generation that came out of Egypt died in the wilderness. It was Moses who finally led this new generation to the Plains of Moab in victory over the two kings east of Jordan. It was Moses who actually apportioned the land east of Jordan to the tribes of Reuben, Gad, and part of Manasseh.

The opening statement, "These are the words," is significant in the light of recent studies of ancient documents. According to Meredith Kline this is an introductory formula used during the second millennium B.C.[1] This seems to have been the normal way in which to introduce a written agreement made between a king and his subject in Mosaic times. Moses, through his training in Egypt, very likely had personal knowledge of treaty patterns prevailing throughout the Fertile Crescent at that time.

THE WILDERNESS JOURNEY (1:6—3:29)

Moses begins with a review of the journey from Mount Horeb to Transjordania. Although the distance from Horeb to Paran from where they should have entered Canaan was only an eleven-day journey, the Israelites had actually spent over thirty-eight years in wilderness wanderings. Now when they were once more on the verge of entering Canaan, Moses solemnly confronts them with a review of the past. With a definite purpose he selects certain events for their consideration.

THE KADESH CRISIS (1:6-46)

Moses does not review what happened at Horeb. Much of what God revealed to Moses at Horeb is recorded in the books of Exodus, Leviticus, and Numbers. He begins with the explicit command by God to enter and possess the land of Canaan which God had promised to the Hebrew patriarchs, 1:8. Repeatedly, Moses refers to this covenant promise (Gen 22:16-18) to give them the land of Canaan (cf. Deu 1:35; 4:31; 6:10, 18, 23; 7:8, 12; 8:1, 18; 9:5; 10:11; 11:9, 21; 13:17; 19:8; 26:3, 15; 28:11; 29:13; 30:20; 31:7, 20-23; 34:4).

Officers and judges had been appointed at Horeb as sug-

gested by Jethro (Ex 18:17-22). In Egypt they had work-
ed as slaves under taskmasters. As a nation of free men,
the officers were responsible with captains as subordinates
to insure justice for all. The Israelites as well as the
strangers were to be treated with equal fairness. Even
though justice issued from God, these judges were charged
with making decisions. Consequently, men of wisdom and
repute were selected for this responsibility of executing
judgment.

Humanitarianism was a distinctive characteristic of the
Mosaic law. In contrast to the Babylonian Code of Hammurabi and the conditions in Egypt as experienced by the
Israelites, this provision offered aid to all who might be
subject to oppression or exploitation. Among God-fearing
people, the justice and righteousness of God should permeate the relationships of members of society.

"Go up, take possession" (1:21) had been the advice
of Moses when they arrived at Kadesh-barnea after their
eleven-day journey from Horeb. The Hebrew word *yārash*
occurs over fifty times in Deuteronomy, and means "take
possession of," "to subdue," or "dispossess," and generally
applies to property or land. The Israelites were to claim
and possess what God had promised. They were admonished not to be afraid or discouraged.

Moses assented to their request to send spies. The result of hearing the majority report was discouragement,
rebellion, and finally God's judgment. Consequently that
generation did not enter Canaan but was doomed to die
in the wilderness.

Did the Israelites at Kadesh-barnea have a reasonable
basis to believe that they could overpower the Canaanites
and possess the land? Moses reminded them (1:30-31)
that God had cared for them as a father cares for his son.

God had guided them in visible manifestation of fire by night and cloud by day. On the basis of this experience since they left Egypt the Israelites should have believed God. Proper fear or reverence for God at this time should have been exemplified by their trusting God to enable them to possess the land of Canaan. Even though this was reasonable on the basis of their experiences, they failed to move forward to conquer the land.

God's people today who claim to believe in Jesus Christ as their Saviour have a reasonable basis to trust God in facing the difficulties of life. The individual who has been turned "from darkness to light, and from the power of Satan unto God" and has received "forgiveness of sins" (Ac 26:18) has experienced a transformation effected by supernatural power. It is this divine source that is available to every God-fearing person as he encounters situations which seem impossible from the natural perspective. Today's Christian may fail to advance in God's plan for him, even as that generation of Israelites failed through rebellion and discouragement to possess Canaan.

Moses speaks freely of the wrath of God as well as the love of God throughout Deuteronomy. The attribute of divine wrath is also explicitly mentioned by Jesus (Jn 3:36) and by Paul (Ro 1:18). The rebellious spirit of that generation was subjected to the wrath of "a jealous God" (Ex 20:5), lest the nation be entirely ruined.

Joshua and Caleb were excluded from this judgment since they "wholly followed the Lord" (1:36; cf. Num 14:24; Jos 14:8-9). In a minority report they advised that with God's help the Israelites could occupy the land (Num 13:30; 14:6-9). They were assured of entrance into Canaan.

Disobedience had dire consequences even for Moses,

who not only was their leader but also prophet and mediator in God's revelation to Israel. Through his disobedience —even though it was caused by the rebellious attitude of the Israelites—Moses was denied entrance into Canaan and the leadership was transferred to Joshua. Moses was primarily accountable to God and then to the people. God does not overlook disobedience even by those who are used in His service.

The rebellious Israelites at Kadesh made an abortive attempt to enter Canaan (1:41-46). Willingness to go after their first rebellion did not atone for their sin. Their attempt to conquer the Canaanites in their own strength made them keenly aware of the reality of divine judgment. For that generation there was no escape from death in the wilderness during the next thirty-eight years (cf. Num 15-19).

The sovereignty of God over the nations is apparent in the boundaries determined for various nations. Although this friendliness shown to the Moabites and Ammonites is characteristic of patriarchal and Mosaic cultures, the Israelites were given explicit instructions to continue to spare these nations. Although David later conquered the Edomites, he did not dispossess them (2 Sa 8:14).

The advance against the Amorites was also an explicit command of God (3:2). Furthermore, the Israelites were assured of success in this holy war. The Amorites had degraded into such idolatry that their time for judgment had ripened (cf. Gen 15:16). Although generation after generation had been exposed to the opportunities to turn to God, the cup of iniquity had at last been filled to the point of divine judgment. The Israelites under the command of God executed this judgment as indicated in the next chapter.

ISRAEL'S RELATIVES (2:1-23)

Once again the Israelites had been commanded to move on. Being refused passage through Edomite territory they were compelled to circuit to the south and then northward to Transjordania (2:8; cf. Num 20:20). Although Edom blocked Israel's passage through Seir because they were afraid of them, the Israelites were instructed not to harm them. They were not to take Edomite territory, since this land had been given to Esau's descendants for their inheritance (cf. Gen 36). Actually, the Edomites were assured of a relatively favored position in the congregation of Israel (Deu 23:7-8).

Next en route were the Moabites (2:9-18). As descendants of Lot, the Moabites were also a privileged people whom the Israelites were divinely forbidden to dispossess. The territory south of the Arnon River and east of the Dead Sea down to the Zered River was allotted to the Moabites by Yahweh, the Great King of Israel.

Marching along the Zered and then north to the Arnon, the Israelites also made contact with the Ammonites who were located east and north of the Moabites. The Ammonites too were descendants of Lot, whose territorial rights were to be respected by Israel (2:19-23).

CONQUEST AND DIVISION (2:24—3:29)

Moses continues his historical survey, pointing out that under his leadership they had actually defeated two Amorite kings and occupied their territory. The Amorites had extended from Canaan east across the Jordan and had taken possession of this territory, which apparently had not been included in the land of promise. When the Israelites made peace overtures to Sihon, the Amorite king of Heshbon, and were refused, they conquered his cities and subdued the land north to the Jabbok (2:24-37).

Next they advanced northward to defeat Og, the King of Bashan, and occupied his territory extending Israel's possession on the east of Jordan northward to Mount Hermon (3:1-17). This newly conquered land had been assigned to the tribes of Reuben, Gad, and half the tribe of Manasseh, (Num 32), with the provision that their men would aid the rest of the nation of Israel in the conquest of the promised land west of the Jordan.

Moses pointed out to Joshua a reasonable basis for his faith in believing that the Israelites would conquer the rest of Palestine (3:21). Since God had manifested His power in successfully conquering and occupying the eastern bank of Jordan, they had reason to believe that God would do the same as they crossed the Jordan. Although Moses himself was only permitted to view the promised land from Pisgah's height, he was told to charge and publicly encourage Joshua to assume the leadership (3:28).

THE RIGHT WAY (4:1-49)

Lessons were to be learned from the mistakes of the previous generation as well as from divine guidance. Moses stresses the uniqueness of God's revelation to them and their responsibility.

WISDOM IN PRACTICE (4:1-8)

Moses issues a call for obedience. "Statutes" (permanent rules of conduct prescribed by proper authority, usually in written form for guiding the individual and society) and "judgments" or ordinances (judicial decisions which serve as future precedents for the guidance of judges) are repeatedly emphasized by Moses as crucially significant. Life itself, as well as occupation and possession of the land, are dependent on obedience to these rules and regulations.

Consider the emphasis here that this is the word of God. Consequently they are not to add to or take away from these divine commands. Jesus struck a similar chord in His teaching (cf. Mt 5:17-19; 15:6). Note also the final warning in the book of Revelation (22:18-19). Although circumstances required modification of some Mosaic enactments in subsequent development, no change in basic principle should be given consideration.

This law that Moses set before the Israelites was to be observed "in the land whither ye go to possess it" (4:5). It would serve as a guide in their manner of life for coming generations as God's covenant people. The ceremonial and judicial regulations were of a temporal nature and were terminated with the fuller revelation in the coming of Jesus (cf. Heb 9:1-15).

Unique in the history of mankind is this revelation of God through Moses. The eternal principles of holiness, justice, and truth issued not from man but from God, and therefore the Israelites would be known as wise people if they lived in accordance with this revelation. The basic principles given in this law were consequently not only for the Israelites but also for all people who reflect a vital relationship with God. Note the frequent use Jesus and the New Testament writers make of Deuteronomy (cf. Mt 4:4, 7, 10; Ro 13:9; and others).

THE FEAR OF GOD (4:9-31)

The basic lesson for Israel to learn at Horeb was to fear and reverence God. They had heard God's voice but they had seen no form nor likeness of God, only an appearance of fire (4:11, 15, 24). Consequently, they could not make a likeness of this God in any manner. What they had seen of God by way of manifestation through fire, and what they had heard—this they were to teach their children. This reverence and respect for God who is a consuming fire was to be conveyed to the succeeding generations.

Any attempt to make a material representation of God was forbidden. Worship of idols or of nature would precipitate God's wrath in subjecting them to exile. There they would indeed serve and worship idols which were the work or product of man's hands. They should never forget the fact that God who had revealed Himself through voice and fire at Horeb had redeemed them from Egyptian slavery. This God they should always revere and respect. Likewise, they should make this God—along with proper respect and reverence for Him—known to their children.

Israel had entered into a contractual agreement with God at Horeb. This covenant (4:13) is mentioned twenty-six times in subsequent passages in Deuteronomy. God extended His grace to Israel in entering into a vital relationship with them, and the Israelites ratified this agreement (Ex 24:1-8). As was customary in Mosaic times two copies of this covenant were provided on two tablets of stone. The law given at Sinai is properly a suzerainty treaty rather than a legal code, and Deuteronomy is a covenant-renewal document. Consequently it has some modification or modernizations of the code given originally. This was customary in the renewal of such treaties.

THE UNIQUENESS OF GOD (4:32-40)

Israel's God and Israel's relationship with God were unique. No one had ever heard the voice of God and seen the fiery manifestation of God and lived. Israel had been redeemed and had been the recipient of God's revelation, in which they heard a voice from heaven and had seen a manifestation of fire on earth (4:36). Why had God revealed Himself? Because God loved the patriarchs and chose to redeem Israel.

This God who is unequaled and manifested Himself in an unprecedented revelation to Israel in redemptive power, is to be given careful respect and reverence through obedience. This response of obedience will prolong life and blessings for the Israelites and their children.

THE CIRCUMSTANCES OF MOSES' PROCLAMATION (4:41-49)

In connection with this address to his people, Moses cites the fact that three cities east of the Jordan River had been designated as cities of refuge as part of the inheritance God had provided. Likewise, the summary of the Transjordanian conquest provides a conclusion to the historical prologue and an introduction to the emphasis of their covenant relationship in the following address.

The time and place are carefully stated for this second discourse by Moses, which begins with 5:1 and ends with 26:19. The basic commandments are given and elaborated in chapters 5-11 and the detailed delineations in 12-26. Throughout, Moses adds warnings and admonitions concerning the relationship that had been established and was to be maintained between the two contracting parties, God and the Israelites. Chapters 5-26 constitute the stipulations when the book of Deuteronomy is viewed as a covenant-renewal similar to ancient Near Eastern vassal treaties.

2

THE LOVE RELATIONSHIP
(5:1—11:32)

WHAT DID GOD ACTUALLY DEMAND of Israel in their relationship with Him? What did Moses, who was the mediator and the prophet through whom Israel's religion was revealed, emphasize as crucially important in Israel's religious life? In these chapters Moses publicly proclaims what primarily matters to the new generation in their total pattern of living.

ISRAEL'S LORD GOD (5:1-33)

The Decalogue—or Ten Commandments—constitutes the essence of God's revelation at Horeb when the covenant relationship was established and ratified. All other stipulations and additions revealed subsequently through the prophets were based on this primary revelation through Moses.

Consider also the implications of the Decalogue for the Christian. Jesus emphasized these commandments as binding upon the conduct of believers when He instructed the young ruler to observe them if he wanted to inherit or obtain eternal life (Mt 19:16-22; Mk 10:17-22). Con-

sequently anyone who professes to believe in Jesus Christ
can hardly ignore the Decalogue. Paul repeats the commandments pertaining to interpersonal relationships in
describing how believers should love one another (Ro
13:8-10).

Moses appeals to his hearers by the words *hear* and
observe, that is, be careful to keep and obey that which
God requires. They have entered into a covenant with
God; therefore they should be sensitive to what God expects.

Although somewhat modified, as Moses is now speaking in an advisory manner, the ten commandments given
here are essentially the same as recorded in Exodus 20.
The style is more homiletical in Deuteronomy.

Moses makes them keenly aware of the fact that God
"talked with you face to face in the mount out of the midst
of the fire" (5:4). This was God's revelation in word to
them and not merely their interpretation of God's manifestation. God had communicated to them in intelligible
words which they had understood, with Moses present as
a witness. The Israelites were not left to their own resources
to state what God required, but the essence of what God
wanted them to know was given in the spoken word and
recorded on tablets of stone for them and their children.

First and foremost was God's vital relationship with
Israel. God exists and has projected Himself into the
temporal affairs of the Israelites in redemption. God identified Himself as the one who had redeemed them out of
Egyptian bondage. God had initiated a relationship with
them by freeing them from slavery. His grace, mercy, love,
and power had been extended into their lives in a realistic
experience. This recognition of God in His redemptive
power was basic in any relationship with God.

For the Christian — or New Testament believer — the

acknowledgment of Christ as Redeemer is essential in initiating a vital relationship with God. Every other consideration in the Christian life issues out of this experience of the supernatural redeeming experience through Jesus Christ from the slavery of sin.

The rest of the commandments have significance as they have a bearing on the relationship established in the first one. Moses' elaboration of the first commandment in chapters 6-11 indicates that when this vital relationship between God and man is fulfilled in a man's life, the rest of the requirements will normally fall into place.

The Decalogue (5:6-21) may be analyzed as a suzerainty treaty as follows: preamble (5:6a); historical prologue (5:6b, 15a); general commandments (5:7); specific stipulations (5:8, 9a, 11a, 12-14a, 15b, 16a, 17-21); curses (5:9b, 11b); blessings (5:10, 16b).

God does not tolerate other gods. In Ur and Haran the contemporary generation of Abraham had worshiped in temples dedicated to the moon. In Egypt the sun was worshiped at Heliopolis (On). Canaan, as discovered by archeological excavations, was abounding in pagan deities represented by figurines exhibiting crude and exaggerated sexual features. These pagan rites and ceremonies, including snake worship, sacred prostitution, and child sacrifice, stood in sharp contrast to the Mosaic law. The warning against graven images and other gods was very appropriate for the Israelites, who were delivered from the pagan culture of Egypt and about to enter the land of Canaan with its licentious Baal rites.

Israel's God could not be represented by any image. The golden calf worship (Ex 32) could not in any way serve as a means of acknowledging the true God. The ark of the covenant with its cherubim did not materially represent Israel's God, even though the pillar of cloud by day and the pillar of fire by night hovered over it in the midst of Israel's camp.

Our Lord Jesus Christ demands the same exclusive standard for discipleship of His followers as God did of the Israelites (cf. Mt 16:24-27; Mk 8:34-38; Lk 9:23-26). He will tolerate no rival claim to one's affections (Lk 14:26-33).

God's name was not to be used in vain. God is a holy God and His name is holy (Ps 111:9; Lk 1:49). Consider what Jesus said about God's name (Jn 17:6, 26), and also that He taught us to pray "hallowed be thy name."

The Sabbath day was to be observed as a holy day in honor of God. Since being freed from Egyptian bondage, the Israelites were to rest from their labors on the seventh day. In this way it signified for the Israelites the covenant sign or seal of their redemption and continual sanctification (Ex 31:13-17; Eze 20:12). God had redeemed them; therefore they were to honor God in a special way on this day. Every week they were to be reminded of their redemption from slavery as they observed the Sabbath as a holy day.

For the Christian the observance of one day in seven is also associated with his redemption (Ro 4:25). Since Christ's resurrection for our justification occurred on the first day of the week, it has been the practice of Christians since then to observe it as a holy day (cf. Rev 1:10 concerning John's vision on "the Lord's day").

God expected His people to honor their parents. Next to God, each individual in the normal circumstances of life owes his very existence to his parents. Consequently, in the realm of human relationships, parents are to be honored and respected. Paul indicates that this is the first commandment with a promise attached (Eph 6:2). Note also the teaching and example of Jesus on allegiance to God and to parents (Mt 10:37; 19:29; Lk 2:49-51; Jn 19:26-27).

The last five commandments of the Decalogue involve human relationships. All are stated in negative terms. None of these would restrict man's pattern of living if he would observe the simple but comprehensive commandment, "Thou shalt love thy neighbor as thyself: I am the LORD" (Lev 19:18).

Life must be treated with reverence. It is God who determines the beginning and end of life. It is God who ordains judges, rulers, and governments to administer justice concerning those who take the lives of others (cf. Gen 9:4-6; Deu 17:2-7; 19:12, Ro 13:4). Animal life may be taken as God's provision for man's sustenance (Gen 9:2-3), but man is accountable to God for taking another man's life (Gen 4:10; cf. Deu 21:1-9).

Marriage was instituted by God (Gen 2:23-25; Mt 19:4-6). Note the detailed regulations given for guarding the sanctity of this human relationship (Deu 21-25). God's love for Israel (Ho 2:14-20) and Christ's love for His church (Eph 5:23-32; cf. Mt 9:15; Jn 3:29) are spoken of in terms of a matrimonial bond. Lack of love for God is compared to adultery (Deu 31:16; Is 50:1; Jer 3:1; Eze 23; and Ja 4:4).

Stealing, bearing false witness, and covetousness impinge upon the rights of others and therefore are not to be characteristic of the life of a God-fearing individual. Possession of property has divine sanction (Deu 8:17-18; 1 Co 4:7). Truth is important in relationship with God as well as with man (Eph 4:17-32). Covetousness, which pertains to the heart condition rather than the visible deeds represented in stealing and slander, is also forbidden. Note Paul's discussion of these commandments in Romans 13:8-

14. These basic rules continue to be one of God's means of revealing the sins and deeds of the flesh (Ro 7:7-14; Gal 3:19-24; 5:13-26).

Having restated the Decalogue, Moses reviews the circumstances in which God revealed this agreement at Horeb (5:22-33). God spoke and provided written copies of His message. The people who heard and saw God's manifestation requested Moses to be their representative with the assurance that they would be fully obedient (v. 27).

God took note of their commitment to be obedient. In verse 29 there is expressed the concern of a loving compassionate God that the Israelites would sincerely follow through in their commitment and obey the commandments, so that they and their children would prosper.

With the memory of this awesome unique experience, Moses appeals to the new generation to give their most serious consideration to what God expects of them. At stake is prosperity and life in the land of promise (5:32-33).

EXCLUSIVE DEVOTION (6:1-25)

Moses, as mediator between God and Israel, had been charged by God with the responsibility to teach the commandments to the Israelites (5:31). Moses' concern is that successive generations may maintain a sensitivity to the conditions that will insure long life and prosperity (6:1-3). Obedience must be a continuous practice if they are to maintain God's favor. Their loyalty has a direct bearing on their tenure in the land.

How could Israel fulfill the requirements of God in a practical manner? Should the Decalogue be considered a list of laws that could be observed in a legalistic manner? Was it possible to achieve a fulfillment of these laws by meeting the demands and then forgetting them? In a prac-

tical way Moses delineates Israel's responsibility as he succinctly states what is essential.

The words of Moses in 6:4-9 with the addition of 11:13-
21 and Numbers 15:37-41 constitute the *Shema,* the great
confession of faith of Judaism. Pious Jews recite this twice
daily in their liturgy. The opening statement expresses the
acknowledgment that God is "the only God." The recognition of other gods is precluded by those who share in this
covenant. With this opening confession, the individual
takes on him the yoke of the kingdom or the sovereignty
of God, and then proceeds to assume the obligations of the
specific commandments.

First and foremost of all that was essential for the
Israelite was an unreserved, wholehearted commitment,
expressed in love for God. Since this relationship involved
the divine being who could not be physically seen nor
materially represented in any likeness similar to pagan
gods, it was essential that the Israelites should reflect this
relationship in daily life. Consequently, they were to teach
their children by talking about God in their everyday con-
versations and by placing the divine commandments in
written form before them in the home. Special warning
was expressed that in time of prosperity, after they occupied the land of Canaan, they would have a tendency
to forget God. The consideration of other gods was absolutely forbidden and would precipitate God's wrath against
them (6:4-15).

The Israelites were not to test or tempt God by doubting
His presence among them (Ex 17:7). Diligence in living
up to this wholehearted commitment would assure them of
successful occupation of the land (6:16-19).

In response to the questions of succeeding generations
concerning these commandments, the simple answer should
be that God had redeemed them through His mighty acts

from Egyptian enslavement (6:20-25). Practical righteousness consisted of reflecting in daily life their conformity to
what God required of them. On the basis of 6:5, it may
be summarized: Love God wholeheartedly and exclusively.

How can a realistic consciousness of God be maintained
and transmitted from generation to generation? This was
of deep concern to Moses as he spoke to the people about
to enter Canaan, and it should be equally important for
the Christian in our day. The Israelites had numerous
external things—signs on their hands, frontlets or phylac-
teries on their foreheads (6:8), scripture verses on their
doorposts and gates (6:9), or tassels on their garments
(Num 15:37-41)—to remind them of God and their responsibility to love Him without reserve. In the course of
time these external things became an end rather than a
means to an end. This was legalism. They became more
concerned about the careful observance of minutiae and
neglected the basic desire of God expressed in the statement: "Love the LORD your God."

In modern times it is possible to observe as mere rituals
practices such as reading Scripture, praying, attending
church, and tithing without exemplifying a wholehearted
devotion to God. As praiseworthy as such habits are, it is
important that the person who confesses to be a Christian
be known for his unreserved commitment of love for God
instead of his legalistic observance of certain practices in
his life.

GOD'S CHOSEN PEOPLE (7:1-26)

How should the Israelites relate to the inhabitants of
Canaan? The instructions were plainly given. The Israelites
were divinely commanded to destroy these people and
occupy their land. Intermarriage was forbidden lest the
Israelites be led into idolatry. The altars and idols were to

be destroyed. In God's economy it was time for judgment (7:1-5). The iniquity of the inhabitants of Canaan, which had not reached the point of divine judgment in the days of Abraham (Gen 15:16), was now so great that God commanded His people to show no mercy.

The Israelites were God's chosen, special, holy people because God bestowed His love upon them. They did not merit this, but God fulfilled His promise made to the patriarchs by delivering them from Egypt. God's goodness would continue toward them if they responded by loving Him (7:6-11). God's love—expressed in their prosperity, protection from diseases, and continued mercy—would distinguish Israel from all other nations if they implemented these divine commandments in their daily lives (7:12-15).

The Israelites had no reasonable basis to be afraid of the nations of Canaan. The fact that God had delivered Israel from the mighty pharaoh of Egypt was the basis for belief that God would also enable them to defeat the petty Canaanite kings. The wasp or hornet (7:20) may have inflicted a fatal sting under certain conditions. But whether Moses spoke of the hornet literally or as a metaphor for some military power, the message of assurance was that God would cause their enemies to panic before them in the conquest of Canaan. They were to destroy them and their gods which were an abomination to the God of Israel (7:16-26).

God-fearing people today are not under the divine command to destroy idolatry and idolators as the Israelites were when they entered Canaan. Christians, however, need to evaluate their involvement in contemporary culture and associations as it affects their exclusive devotion to God (cf. Ro 12:1-2; 2 Co 6:14—7:1). God's people are to exert a positive influence Godward rather than be ensnared by godlessness in the world.

LESSON FROM HISTORY (8:1-20)

Remember is a key word used by Moses repeatedly as he speaks to the Israelites. In this chapter he uses it twice (8:2 and 18). They are to recall again and again what God has done for them. Note the context of the other usages of this admonition (5:15; 7:18; 9:7; 15:15; 16:3, 12; 24:9, 18; 25:17; and 3:27). Closely related to this was the warning "not to forget," used three times in this chapter (8:11, 14, and 19) and repeatedly throughout Deuteronomy (4:9, 23, 31; 6:12; 9:7; 24:19; 25:19; 26:13).

Although the daily supply of manna had become commonplace, the Israelites were never to forget that this and the fact that their clothes never wore out (8:4-5) were a supernatural provision. The daily manifestation of divine sustenance was to teach them that man does not live by bread alone. Consider Jesus' use of this verse in His temptation (Mt 4:4).

In Palestine the supply of food would be less supernatural as they ate of abundant crops, mined resources of iron and copper, and prospered with enlarged flocks and herds. There as they developed the natural resources they would face the tendency to forget about God as the source of all things.

Discipline was a crucial factor in the experience of the Israelites. Without God's help the Israelites could not have freed themselves from Egyptian bondage. When they suffered hunger God supplied them with manna (8:16). When drought was about to overtake them water supernaturally flowed from the hard or flinty rock. These humbling experiences represented God's discipline, but it was in the context of a father-son relationship. Moses interprets the past for the Israelites and reminds them that they owe their very existence to God.

In times of wealth and affluence, people are apt to become self-sufficient, independent, and even arrogant. Moses pinpoints this attitude in "My power and the might of mine hand hath gotten me this wealth" (8:17). This represents "forgetting God." This precipitates judgment and destruction even for the Israelite.

Ability to achieve is given by God. A God-fearing person, whether an Israelite in Old Testament times or a Christian in the New Testament era, must always be conscious that all abilities are a divine endowment. Consequently, man dare not credit himself with success. Daily food and sustenance should continuously be accepted with thankfulness to God for His provision. Jesus taught us the attitude of daily dependence when He instructed us to pray "Give us this day our daily bread." A Christian can no more afford to forget God than the Israelite could in his daily life.

SINFUL ISRAEL (9:1—10:11)

Moses reminds the Israelites of their sinfulness at Horeb (9:7-21; cf. Ex 32). They had made a molten image of a bull calf while Moses was representing them on the mountain where God revealed Himself. By this action they were divinely labeled as a stiffnecked, stubborn, or headstrong people (cf. 9:13 and Ex 33:5). When Moses saw the idolatry of his people, he was so enraged that he broke the two stone tablets, symbolizing by this action the breaking of the covenant. But through the fervent intercession of Moses, the Israelites at that time were spared the judgment and wrath of God. Even Aaron needed the prayerful intervention of Moses.

Moses reviews several other incidents for them to impress upon them that they were a rebellious people who had incurred the wrath of God (9:22-23). At Taberah

(Num 11:1-3), Massah (Ex 17:1-7), and Kibroth-hat-taavah (Num 11:4-34) they had provoked God's anger. At Kadesh-barnea they failed God in their lack of faith and disobedience (Num 13-14).

Moses charges the Israelites with having been "rebellious against the LORD from the day that I knew you" (9:24). Moses made his intercessory appeal to God on the fact that Israel, having been redeemed from Egypt, was God's inheritance, and the fact that they were descendants of the patriarchs (9:26-27). The Israelites had no righteousness to their credit, but only stubbornness, wickedness, and sin (9:27). They were guilty of sin and unrighteous before God.

Fortunately, God had listened to Moses' intercession and had dealt in mercy with the Israelites who had broken the covenant. The tablets of stone with the written Decalogue were replaced and stored in the ark which had been with them ever since that time as the symbol of God's presence in their midst (10:1-5).

Provision was also made for the continual care of the ark by appointing the tribe of Levi to this responsibility. Most important was the fact that the Levites were "to stand before the LORD to minister unto him, and to bless in his name" (10:8-9). Even when Aaron died (Num 20:22-29) the continuation of the priestly ministry was assured in the appointment of Eleazar. The Levites were not assigned any tribal inheritance as the other tribes were, so that they could serve throughout the entire nation.

Because of Moses' intercession—and not because of their righteousness—the Israelites were now encamped on the banks of the Jordan, ready to enter the land of promise (10:10-11).

The Israelites had no merit of their own on which to claim the right to enter Canaan. Neither does the Christian have any righteousness whereby he can claim anything before God. As Moses effectively made intercession for Israel, so Jesus Christ intercedes for those who have been redeemed from the bondage of sin. Salvation for the Israelites as well as for the Christian is provided by God, and not based on man's righteousness.

MOSES' APPEAL TO COMMITMENT (10:12—11:32)

What does God expect of His people? What is essential in their relationship with God? Reverence, love, and wholehearted obedience—these are repeated for emphasis (cf. 6:5, 13, 24).

Who is this God whom the Israelites are to love sincerely and without reservation? He is the Lord of the cosmos, He is God above all that are called gods, He is the righteous Judge, He rules supreme over all nature and history.

What has this God done for them? He has loved and chosen their forefathers the patriarchs, He has given Israel covenant status, He has manifested Himself in helping the orphans, widows, and strangers, He has multiplied the Israelites as the stars of the heavens.

Moses gives two explicit instructions to the Israelites who are on the verge of entering Canaan.

1. "Circumcise therefore the foreskin of your heart" (10:16).
2. "Love ye therefore the sojourner" (10:19).

Moses does not refer to physical circumcision, which was the sign of the Abrahamic covenant (Gen 17). Even this had not been observed during the period of wilderness wanderings but was reinstituted after they entered Canaan (Jos 5:2-9). The language was clear and explicit that Moses here referred to the circumcision of the heart—a spiritual relationship Godward (cf. Lev 26:40-41; Jer 4:4;

9:25; Ro 2:29). It was with "all thy heart" that they
were admonished to love God. All things that might restrict, interfere with, or negate a total devotion to God
were to be cut away (circumcised). Nothing should mar
this vertical relationship established in the covenant.

The horizontal responsibility was equally distinct and
could hardly be misinterpreted. Love for the stranger or
neighbor is basic to all other obligations man has in this
life (cf. Lev 19:9-18). The social or humanitarian obligations issue out of man's relationship with God. The Israelites were to love others because God had loved them. Their
capacity to love others was dependent on their realization
of God's love for them when they were strangers in Egypt.
The vertical love relationship Godward is a prerequisite for
the horizontal involvement manward. God loves the stranger, the widow, the orphan; therefore man—if he loves
God—is under obligation to love his fellowman. God is
concerned about justice and righteousness; therefore
man—if he loves God—must be concerned about the just
treatment of his neighbors.

God's people were to be known for their solicitude for
those people whose social and economic position exposed
them to exploitation and oppression. The Mosaic law is
permeated by a profound humanitarian spirit and stands
in unique contrast to the Babylonian code of Hammurabi
and the Assyrian and Hittite law codes of that day. In
the latter, the human relationships did not reflect the vital
consciousness of God so basic to the life of Israel.

These two responsibilities, complete love for God and
love for neighbor, constituted the essence of what God
required of man. This was the core of God's message to
man as revealed through Moses at Horeb. Not legalism,
not ritual, not external minutiae of religious observances,
not a legalistic observance of the Decalogue, or a system

of negatives and positive principles or creeds—none of these was basic. Rather, Moses emphasized a vital relationship with God as fundamental to all other issues in life. Second to this was a genuine love relationship with fellowman.

Moses delineates their responsibility of heartfelt love as he anticipates the entrance of the Israelites into Canaan (11:1-32). Briefly he states the facts so well known to them. They know about God's

1. Chastisement or discipline (11:2)
2. Mighty acts in deliverance (11:2-4)
3. Sustaining power (11:5)
4. Judgment (11:6)

This knowledge of the past provided a basis for projecting into the future.

The promise for the future was clearly stated. They are assured that if they love God and obey Him,

1. They will possess the land (11:8)
2. They will live long in Canaan (11:9, 18-21)
3. God will care for the land, providing rain (11:10-17)
4. God will expel the inhabitants of Canaan (11:22-25)

The conclusion of Moses in this appeal for total love and commitment Godward is unmistakably clear (11:26-32). The choice is up to them. God's blessing awaits them if they listen and obey, but God's curse is their lot if they ignore Him.

The epitome of God's requirement for the Israelites as given by Moses (10:12—11:32) is basically important for the Christian. Jesus pointed to the command to love God as the greatest commandment and love for neighbor as the second. These two commandments not only constitute the essence of the entire Old Testament revelation but also provide the basis for eternal life (cf. Mt 22:37-39; Mk 12:29-31; Lk 10:27).

Since Jesus Christ was the climax of God's revelation to offer whosoever will the opportunity to respond to God's love, the option for today is one of faith in Jesus Christ. Jesus Himself taught that the one who places his faith in God's only Son does not come under judgment or the wrath of God, but he who does not believe in Jesus Christ is under judgment already (Jn 3:18). For the Israelite it was either blessing or curse; for man today it is either eternal life in Christ or God's eternal wrath.

3

INSTRUCTIONS IN PRACTICAL LIVING FOR A GOD-RELATED PEOPLE

(12:1—26:19)

HAVING ELABORATED on the foundation principles of the Sinai covenant, Moses now delineates the practical applications for life in Canaan. When they have settled throughout the land instead of being encamped around the tabernacle, their worship will be modified. Instead of the supernatural supply of manna, the Israelites will plant and harvest. Many problems will develop as they encounter the contemporary culture and especially the religion of the Canaanites. As Moses anticipates these, he emphasizes the importance for the Israelites to live as God's holy people. Justice and righteousness are to characterize their relationships with one another. Brotherly love is to permeate their domestic and social involvements. Immediate entry into Canaan is anticipated in all that follows (cf. 12:10).

WORSHIP OF GOD IN CANAAN (12:1—16:17)

Changes and adjustments are necessary as the Israelites move across the Jordan River to occupy the land of Canaan. When all the tribes were encamped under Moses' leadership around the tabernacle, the Israelites to a certain extent did what seemed "right to each in his own eyes" (12:8).

Slaughter of animals for any purpose was limited to the tabernacle entrance, lest any one associate the killing of animals with idolatrous practices according to Egyptian customs. Now that the Israelites anticipate living in settled conditions throughout the land of Canaan, Moses gives instructions concerning the worship of God and daily life adjusted to the new conditions.

SANCTITY IN WORSHIP (12:1—14:21)

Idolatrous shrines were to be demolished (12:2-3). These are identified by the Hebrew term *meqōmôt* and not *bāmôt* which is the designation for "high places." The fact that *bāmôt* does not occur in chapters 12-26 negates the theory that Deuteronomy was written during Josian times (6th century B.C.) to prohibit the use of "high places," the term frequently found in the accounts of Josiah's reform (2 Ki 23:5-20; 2 Ch 33:3, 17, 19; 34:3). At these shrines —on mountains, hills, and under green trees—the Canaanites had built altars, and pillars to perform their rites in sacrificing their sons and daughters to their gods (12:31). God hated these abominations and had already given explicit instructions to the Israelites to kill the Canaanite idolaters (7:1-6). Here in this context where the central sanctuary is emphasized, the divine command is repeated that God expects the Israelites to destroy these idolatrous shrines. The reason or purpose is clearly stated (12:29-31). If the Israelites take residence among these pagan shrines, they may be tempted to use them as places of worship. Pagan rites and ceremonies, which were expressly forbidden (14:1), dare not be tolerated by the Israelites in any form. These could not be used under any circumstances for religious purposes. Therefore they were commanded to destroy and remove them without exception.

The Israelites were to worship at the "place which the LORD your God shall choose" (12:5, 10, 18, 21). Various places became centers of worship after they settled in Canaan. Moses instructs them to erect an altar at Mount Ebal for the reading of the law (27:1-8; cf. Jos 8:30-35). Shechem, located between Mount Ebal and Mount Gerizim, continued as a sanctuary, for it was at Shechem that Joshua assembled all Israel before his death for the renewal and updating of the Sinaitic covenant (Jos 24:1-28). Shiloh, where the tabernacle was erected under Joshua (Jos 18:1), continued to be the central place for worship throughout the period of the Judges (Judg 21:19; 1 Sa 1:3; 2:14; 3:21; Ps 78:60; Jer 7:12; 26:6). No mention or inference in Deuteronomy offers any basis for the theory that Jerusalem is in view in the book of Deuteronomy as is advocated by those who suggest a sixth-century date for its writing. Jerusalem was a Jebusite stronghold until the time of David (cf. 2 Sa 7-10).

The tabernacle represented God dwelling among His people (Ex 25:8; cf. also Jn 1:14 and Rev 21:3). The prohibition to choose altars at random (12:13) was timely, since the Israelites might be tempted to use the altars of the Canaanites. Animals which were God's provision for food could be killed in their home communities instead of at the tabernacle as had been the restriction during their encampments (12:13-28; 15:21-23). As God's people they were to recognize blood as the symbol and vital element of life itself, especially in bringing their sacrifices (Lev 17:10-12; cf. Gen 9:4-6). (Note also how this relates to atonement in Lev 16; Heb 9:12-14; 1 Pe 1:18-19; 1 Jn 1:7).

The Levites to whom no territorial allotment was made

similar to the rest of the tribes were to be given proper care among the Israelites (12:17-19). The tithe and share in the offerings was their provision for livelihood.

As they worshiped God in the bringing of their sacrifices, tithes, and offerings, the Israelites were to fellowship as they ate together at the sanctuary and to rejoice before the Lord (12:4-7). This joy was an essential part of their religion as they and their children acknowledged that God had blessed them in their labors. The entire household— sons, daughters, male and female slaves—as well as the Levites were to share in this joy or spiritual blessing.

Severe action was to be taken against any idolater or any Israelite who attempted to promote idolatry (13:1-18). Three examples are cited concerning people who advocate the worship of other gods: false teachers, members in a family, and residents in a city.

A divine test of Israel's love for God was a false prophet (13:3). The fact that he made accurate predictions might suggest that he was a prophet of the Lord, but if he advised idolatry he was to be dealt with severely nevertheless. Israel was to be devoted to God completely, and any religious leader who advised people to consider idolatry was to be executed (13:5). The Mosaic revelation was normative and provided a definite standard by which prophets and prophecy were to be judged as to truth and falsity.

The death penalty was also to be applied within the family unit. Any member of a family—brother, son, daughter, wife, or intimate friend—who secretly tempts people to worship idols is to be stoned to death (13:6-11). No tolerance of idolatry was permitted within the family. In executing capital punishment, the convicting witness was to cast the first stone. Love for family or relatives must not take precedence over exclusive devotion to God (cf. Lk 14:26).

Cities likewise might be confronted with the question of tolerating idolatry through the influence of "base fellows" (ASV and RSV) or "children of Belial" (KJV). Failure in the family to execute such worthless fellows made it possible for them to influence larger population groups congregated in cities. Consequently society at large became involved in these unfortunate developments. Any city that tolerated such idolatry was to be destroyed, including people, cattle, and property. Full investigation was important as a principle of justice preceding punishment. The gravity of permitting such tolerance toward idolatry seems to be emphasized through the instructions that even the property could not be confiscated as the spoils of war but was subject to the ban of total destruction (13:12-18). This prevented the Israelites from such action for the purpose of material gain.

Bodily care and hygienic regulations were also important if they were to live as God's holy people (14:1-21). They were forbidden to mutilate themselves as the heathen did in their mourning rites, thereby defacing the image of God (cf. Lev 19:28; 21:5; 1 Ki 18:28; 1 Co 3:17). Note also the New Testament teaching that the body is the temple of the Holy Spirit (Ro 12:1-2; 1 Co 6:9-20).

The ceremonial and dietary regulations are somewhat arbitrary, but they do convey significant ideas of preventive medicine and hygiene. The animals here specified for food reflect the wilderness area of Israel's sojourn as given in Leviticus 11:2-23 (cf. 14:4b-5 as a supplement). Health might be endangered by eating pigs, which even in modern conditions may carry dangerous parasitic organisms. Crustacea or shellfish which often feed on putrefying garbage, and birds feeding on carrion are also prohibited from the Israelite menu. Because of the danger of toxin in animals dying a natural death, the Israelites were to abstain from such, as is the practice in most civilized countries (cf. Lev 17:15).

The ceremonial custom of boiling a kid in its mother's milk is known from the ancient Canaanite tablets found at Ugarit. Such a rite was superstitiously observed by the Canaanites, hoping that through magical acts they could increase fertility and productivity (14:21; Ex 23:19; 34:26).

The instructions and descriptions here as well in Leviticus 11 should not be regarded as strictly scientific. They were practical in the light of contemporary culture and religion and were modified to some extent as Moses speaks to his people. Basic to the total pattern of living was the fact that they were God's holy people (14:1-2, 21).

SHARING GOD'S BLESSINGS (14:22—15:23)

The tithe was to be brought to the central **sanctuary.** Repeatedly, Moses warned them against using the tithe at home and admonished them to share this portion of their income with the Levites who had been substituted for the firstborn among the Israelites to serve in religious ministration assisting the priests, (12:6, 17; 14:22-29; cf. Num 1-8). The giving of the tithe and the offering of animal sacrifices represented an acknowledgment of God. Abraham gave his tithe out of gratitude (Gen 14:20) and Jacob as a token of devotion (Gen 28:22) before the law was given. In this way the Israelites expressed their reverence and respect for God. Sharing this with the Levites, who had no property or inheritance, the Israelites in a practical way provided for the needs of those ministering at the place of worship. Every third year the tithe was to be stored in their local cities for disposition by the Levites (14:28-29; cf. Num 18:26-32).

Joy and rejoicing were to characterize the Israelite

when he appeared at the central sanctuary. Moses emphasizes this repeatedly (12:7, 12, 18; 14:26). Being in the presence of God, bringing an offering from the material blessings God had given to him, and sharing from his abundance with the Levites and others in need, the Israelite had plenty of cause for making this a time of rejoicing. In this manner the Israelite expressed his wholehearted devotion and unreserved response to God who had initially extended His love and mercy toward him.

Care must be taken by the Israelite when he was to bring the firstborn male animals of his flock to dedicate and sacrifice them at the central sanctuary (15:19-23). In so doing the Israelite learned to revere and respect God (14:23). Detailed instruction had been given previously in Exodus (13:2, 11-16; 22:29-30; 34:19-20), Leviticus (27:26-27), and Numbers (18:15-18). The emphasis here is primarily upon the central sanctuary as the place of worship. The animals not meeting the requirements could be eaten at home. Bringing defective animals to the central sanctuary as offerings would have been an act of disrespect for God.

Significant in these instructions is the fact that the family is included with the Israelite as he brings his sacrifice (14:26). In this way the children learned by experience how to revere and worship God. By precept and example the children in the family became aware of the fact that God ought to be acknowledged as the giver and sustainer of life and all its blessings. In this practical way they learned to fear God. Worship of God involved the bringing of a sacrifice as an expression of rejoicing at the sanctuary.

Love toward fellowmen found expression in numerous ways (15:1-18). Every seven years the debts were to be canceled. Additional significance was attached to the Sabbath to remind the Israelites of God's redemptive love manifested in their divine deliverance from Egyptian bondage and slavery (5:15). The release from debts every seven years similarly represented a practical way of expressing their love toward those who had been less fortunate. In this way the poverty-stricken were privileged to share in the material things of the prosperous citizen.

Hebrews enslaved by Hebrews were to be released after six years of service (15:12-18). At the time of release the released individual was to be endowed liberally by his owner who thereby acknowledged God's goodness in freeing Israel from Egyptian bondage and providing continued material blessings for his sustenance. A slave, however, might commit himself voluntarily to a lifetime of service to his master. This commitment was verified by piercing the ear of the slave with an awl (Ex 21:5-6). Note Romans 12:1 in applying this to the Christian life today.

The humanitarian spirit of Mosaic legislation permeates these civic and religious aspects of the Israelite society. It stands in contrast to the lack of dignity accorded to the common man in contemporary cultures of the Mosaic age.

ANNUAL FESTIVALS (16:1-17)

Three annual pilgrimages to the central sanctuary were prescribed: the Feast of Passover and Unleavened Bread, the Feast of Weeks, and the Feast of Tabernacles, 16:1-17 (cf. Ex 12; 23:14; 34:18; Lev 23; Num 28-29). The Passover began on the fourteenth day of the first month Abib (Nisan); the Feast of Weeks was a one-day celebration fifty days later on the sixth of Sivan, the third month; and the Feast of Tabernacles was a seven-day observance beginning on the fifteenth day of the seventh month, Tishri, after the autumn fruit harvest.

The Passover as described here includes the eight-day period beginning with the sacrifice of the lamb as prescribed in Exodus 12:3-11. This was followed by seven days during which sacrifices might be taken from flocks and herds. Throughout this week the Israelites ate unleavened bread. On the eighth day this feast was concluded with a solemn assembly. In this manner the Israelites were annually reminded that once they had been slaves in Egypt and that God had redeemed them through His mighty power. Whereas in Egypt the passover lamb was eaten in the home with the blood applied to the doorposts, the observance in subsequent years centered around the central altar at the tabernacle and later at the temple in Jerusalem. In this way Moses instructed the Israelites in their adaptation to the changing conditions of settlement in Canaan.

Remember, which was a key word at Passover time, is equally important for the Christian when he observes the Lord's Supper. Meditating on Christ's death, he should review his spiritual values and rededicate himself to God (cf. Mt 26:26-30; Lk 22:14-19; 1 Co 11:23-26).

Seven weeks later the Feast of Weeks was observed. This was also identified as the "feast of harvest" (Ex 23:16), or "day of firstfruits" (Num 28:26), and later known by the Greek name "Pentecost." With the grain harvest completed, the Israelites were to observe this one-day festival as a time of rejoicing before their God at the central sanctuary. Again the family was involved, as well as the servants, Levites, immigrants, orphans, and widows. The free-will offering was to be given in proportion to the abundance of blessings as they rejoiced because of the fruitfulness of the land (12:7, 12, 18; 16:10-11, 14-15), and because of the fact that they had been freed from Egyptian slavery (16:12). It was the sharing of these blessings with those in need that made this a very joyous occasion.

The outpouring of the Holy Spirit fifty days after the death of Christ gave significance to this feast day for the Christians (Ac 2:14-18). Note also the prediction made by Joel (2:28-32) and its partial fulfillment on that day and its application in Peter's message.

The third festival to be observed at the central sanctuary was the Feast of Tabernacles, also known as the Feast of Ingathering (16:13-15; cf. Ex 23:16, 34:22; Lev 23:33-43). With the vintage as well as the grain harvests completed, this was the final celebration of each year lasting from Tishri 15-21. Every seventh year at this time the law was read publicly for all to hear (31:9-13). Living in tents or booths during this time at the central sanctuary, the Israelites were reminded from year to year that during the wilderness journey they had lived in tents. At the same time, this last annual festival, held after the culmination of the harvest, was a time of thanksgiving and sharing since the entire community was involved—sons, daughters, male and female servants, Levites, immigrants, fatherless, and widows (16:14). Joy in sharing, thanksgiving, and love permeated the entire celebration.

In concluding this message on the importance of the central place of worship (Deu 12:1—16:17), Moses points out once more that three times a year every male is to make this pilgrimage. Coming with his offering of animals, grain, and vintage, the Israelite repeatedly acknowledges God as the giver and sustainer of life and all its opportunities. With every male required to make this pilgrimage, the entire community was involved. Rejoicing, thanksgiving, sharing—these prevailed during the observance of these festive occasions when the Israelites gathered to worship at the central sanctuary. Shouldn't these characteristics be evident when Christians gather for festive occasions?

JUSTICE IN HUMAN RELATIONS (16:18—21:23)

Since Israel was in a covenant relationship with God as their King, the people of Israel were to reflect the righteousness of God in their administration of justice. Theocratic regulations, unlike that of ordinary states, were entwined with the religious so that the book of the law contained moral and civil as well as cultic stipulations.

DIVINE AUTHORITY (16:18—17:13)

This book of the law was kept at the central sanctuary where priests were in charge. As custodians of the written revelation they had the responsibility to communicate and expound this divine revelation. Consequently they had the dominant judicial voice (cf. 21:5) in the administration of justice. Through the Urim and Thummim they were also the recipients of additional revelation as it was needed in making decisions. Provision was also made for continual revelation through prophets who were to follow Moses (18:15-22 cf. 13:1-5). These prophets were to communicate the messages from their divine King as supplemental instructions were necessary in addition to that which had been revealed through Moses and recorded in the book of the law. Consequently the instructions governing human relationships in civil and moral affairs also contain cultic regulations.

The administration of justice was adapted to the changing times and circumstances in Canaan. Originally, Moses as mediator also served as judge when Israel was encamped at Mount Sinai with assistants as needed (1:12 and Ex 18:13-26). Now judges and other officials were to be appointed in the cities throughout the land. These leaders were instructed to strive for justice (rightness or justness) —"justice, justice shall you follow" (16:20, lit.). Gifts for judges were prohibited lest they be influenced to pervert justice for the sake of material reward (cf. also Lev 19:15).

In Canaan the *'asherah* ("trees," "pillars," or "groves") were associated with oracular verdicts by their gods and goddesses. In Egypt and other neighboring countries the images (*masseboth*) of the numerous gods were used for similar practices. The Israelites had been forbidden in accordance with the first two commandments (Ex 20:3-6; Deu 5:7-10) to allow for any toleration in this respect (16:21-22). The offering requirements in judicial procedure were to express the same respect and reverence for God as was evident in their worship rites (17:1). God was to be acknowledged as the final authority as well as the object of their worship.

Any deviation from the exclusive worship of God was to be dealt with severely. Each Israelite was responsible for eradicating idolatry wherever he encountered it. If a charge of idolatry against an individual was sustained by two or three witnesses, the idolater was to be stoned with the witnesses casting the first stones. This could be done under the jurisdiction of the local elders in the city (17:2-7).

If a case of bloodshed was too difficult for the local judges, then the appeal should be made to those in charge at the central sanctuary. The priest or judge in charge had final authority under God to render a decision which the Israelites were required to accept. Anyone refusing to abide by the verdict given at the central sanctuary was subject to the penalty of death (17:8-13).

CIVIL AND RELIGIOUS LEADERS (17:14—18:22)

Kingship in Israel was permissible but not mandatory. In Egypt the pharaoh considered himself to be a god or empowered to rule by the chief god. Israel had Yahweh their God as their king (cf. Ex 15:18; 19:5-6; Deu 33:5; Judg 8:23). The earthly ruler as king in Israel was required to be subject—as an individual as well as king—to God and the law. Judicial supremacy ultimately was vested in God. The law under the guardianship of the priests at the central sanctuary was so vital to the king in Israel that he was instructed to make a written copy for himself. By his observance of this law he would learn to fear and revere God in his own life. The king was to be an Israelite chosen by God. Israel's king was warned not to conform to the royal courts of surrounding nations by multiplying horses and chariots, multiplying wives, and accumulating to himself an abundance of silver and gold lest his heart deviate from his exclusive devotion to God. In this covenant agreement the king was expected to maintain a wholehearted commitment to and dependence upon God (17:14-20).

Later, when the Israelites requested a king, Samuel anointed Saul. His position, unlike that of rulers of surrounding nations, was that of being captain of God's inheritance or prince over God's people (cf. 1 Sa 9:16 and 10:1). Although David hamstrung his horses (1 Ch 18:4) he did multiply wives and suffered for this violation even though he repented. Solomon seems to have ignored both of these prohibitions and ultimately permitted his numerous wives to bring idolatry into the environs of Jerusalem. This evoked direct warnings from God and prophecies that the kingdom would be torn from the hand of his son (1 Ki 11:1-43).

Priests and prophets were also crucially important in the life of the Israelites (18:1-22). The priests were to receive their support from the people as they brought their offerings, since they did not have a territory allotted to them similar to that of the other tribes. Priesthood within the tribe of Levi was restricted to the descendants of Aaron. Whereas Levites lived in the cities assigned to them throughout Canaan (Jos 21), the priests lived near the central sanctuary where they officiated at the altar. The Levites in their services were subordinate to the priests who had the position of authority and honor. However, both groups—the Levites as well as the priests—were commissioned to instruct the Israelites in their covenant relationship (Deu 33:10 and 2 Ch 15:3). The Levites, which included the priests, were always acknowledged as the ministers of God when they were given a share in the offerings of the Israelites who came to worship.

Moses warned his people that they should not be enticed by the pagan inhabitants of Canaan in their religious practices (18:9-14). The polytheistic rites used by the Canaanites in their worship were offensive to Israel's God, and the participation of the Israelites in these rites would mar the relationship existing between the Israelites and their God. They were forbidden to listen to these pagan soothsayers and diviners.

This condemnation of seeking communication with the departed dead applies to spiritism and the occult in modern life. God-fearing people who have acknowledged Jesus Christ as the fullness of God's revelation and have recognized the ministry of the Holy Spirit need not resort to divination in their concern to know the events of the future.

God had made provision for the Israelites to obtain additional divine guidance as it was needed or desired through the priests by means of the Urim and Thummim (cf. Ex 28:30; Num 27:15-21). To this new generation the additional promise is made that God will send a prophet to speak for God to the people even as Moses did at Horeb (Deu 18:15-22 cf. Ex 20:18-20; Deu 5:22-27).

The "prophet" here seems to signify corporate as well as individual importance—a succession of prophets which were to follow Moses, culminating in the Messiah (Ac 3:22-23; 7:37; Jn 1:21, 25, 43-45; 6:14; 7:40). As Moses served in a mediatorial ministry (18:15), so the prophet would be raised up by God to be the spokesman to reveal God's will to the people as needed.

Death, however, was the punishment for any individual identified as a false prophet. Any individual who spoke in the name of other gods (18:20 and 13:1-5), and proclaimed prophecies which were not fulfilled was not a prophet representing the God of Israel. The words of the true prophet, who was not misleading the people from their wholehearted commitment to God, were regarded by the people as God's word, and therefore as authoritative as that which had been given through Moses. (18:19). In this manner, provision was made for God's communication or divine revelation supplementary to the written law, which was under the custodianship of the priests and Levites.

In the New Testament era, Jesus was recognized as fulfilling the prediction by Moses (cf. Mt 21:11; Lk 7:16; Jn 5:46; Ac 3:22; 7:37; Heb 3:2-6). Jesus was like Moses in numerous ways. He was spared in infancy (Ex 2; Mt 2:13-23); He renounced a royal court (Heb 11:24-27; Phil 2:5-8); had compassion for the people (Num 27:17; Mt 9:36); made intercession (Deu 9:18; Heb 7:25); spoke with God face to face (Ex 34:29-30; 2 Co 3:7); and was mediator of a covenant (Deu 29:1; Heb 8:6-7). The greatest revelation in the Old Testament era came through Moses. This revelation was only surpassed in the coming of Christ, who not only revealed God's message but provided salvation through His death.

PROVISION FOR THE GUILTY (19:1—20:20)

In the administration of justice, further adjustments were necessary as the Israelites anticipated settlement in Canaan. Under the Mosaic provision, the altar became an asylum for someone who killed another person accidentally (Ex 21:12-14). Even as the slaying of animals, which was formerly restricted to the altar at the sanctuary, was decentralized (cf. Deu 12:15), so now the law of asylum is modified. Geographically it would be impractical for many people who were in need of seeking refuge to flee to the central sanctuary. Consequently three cities of refuge were to be established west of the Jordan River (19:1-13), even as three had already been designated to the east of the Jordan River (Num 35:6-15 and Deu 4:41-43).

These cities of refuge became extensions of the central sanctuary altar as asylums, because they were more readily accessible to those who were in need of safety. Although the slaying of animals apart from the central sanctuary lost its ceremonially sacred character, the cities of refuge did not. These six cities of refuge were included in the forty-eight cities assigned to the Levites throughout the land. The need for three additional cities, as verse 9 suggests, must not have materialized, for such cities are not noted anywhere else in the scriptural records. (Since no late writer after the conquest of Canaan would have invented this provision, verse 9 is an evidence of authentic Mosaic authorship.) The elders in the gates of these cities were to render judgment to assure the parties involved of justice, if hatred resulted in bloodshed. Senior members of the society occupied a superior position and were regarded as the local authorities (21:20; 27:1; 29:10; 31:28).

False witness was forbidden where it involved the moving of a landmark or the conviction of a crime in breaking the ninth commandment (19:14-21). Charges could be sustained only on testimony of two or three witnesses. Disputes were to be brought before the priests and judges. These represented Israel's God in the matter of ascertaining justice for the accused as well as the accuser. Perjury was punished according to the principle of *lex talionis* (law of retribution) which was a guarantee of justice rather than a license for vengeance. This rule here applies to the punishment of a false witness, whereas Jesus speaks about the personal conduct of the righteous man (Mt 5:38-42).

Since the priests and judges represented God in the hearing of the charges, the question of bringing false charges became a very serious matter. The priests and judges had a very solemn responsibility and so had the witnesses. Consequently, the one bringing charges faced the possibility that if his charges were proven to be false, he would be subject to the judgment that he had hoped would be given to the one he accused.

The humanitarian principles applicable in warfare under Mosaic law (20:1-20) stand in contrast to the brutality of other nations, especially that of the Assyrians in subsequent periods. Encouragement for battle was provided on the basis that God had delivered the Israelites from Egypt and would still be with His people. The priest represented God as he consecrated the battle against their enemies to the Lord of hosts. Recruiting for the army seemed to be free from compulsion and allowed various causes for exemptions so that nothing could distract the Israelite soldiers from gaining the victory.

When they approached distant cities of enemies, the Israelites were instructed to offer terms of peace to the inhabitants. War was declared and waged only as a last resort. If the latter accepted the terms of peace, then they would become tributary subjects. If these peace overtures were rejected, then the Israelites were assured that God

would grant them the victory in killing the male population and appropriating the spoils of war (20:10-15). Note
here the principle that the proclamation of peace preceded
inevitable judgment (cf. Mt 10:11-15).

The cities of the inhabitants of Canaan, however, were
to be conquered and destroyed so that the Israelites would
not be ensnared by their sinful practices (cf. 7:22-26).
This extreme command of utter destruction was preventa-
tive in purpose 20:20 (cf. Rev 21:27). The trees surrounding any city could be used by the Israelites in conquest as needed, but fruit trees were to be spared for
their sustenance (20:16-20). This also prevented soil
erosion.

RESPONSIBILITY IN THE EXECUTION OF JUSTICE (21:1-23)

That the responsibility for ultimate judicial authority
was vested in the priesthood is clearly affirmed in the instructions given concerning a murdered individual where
the criminal was not identified (21:1-9). The corporate
community was held responsible even as was the case in
the code of Hammurabi centuries earlier. The elders of the
city nearest the slain man were responsible to bring a
heifer to the priest. Since the animal was slain in the field
and not at the altar, the sacrifice was not cultic but judicial.
This distinctly indicates the judicial authority as vested in
the priest. Although the death of the heifer for the unknown murderer did not satisfy justice, it did free the
citizens as well as the bloodstained land from guilt as the
elders confessed their innocence. It also precluded the
possibility of intercity strife, in case any relatives should
seek revenge for the murdered man.

The authority of the home is also delineated in the re-
mainder of this chapter (21:10-23). The husband is defi-
nitely recognized as the head of his household, but he

must give proper recognition to the rights of his wife. When a captive is taken as a wife, the purification acts were to be observed to remove her from the status of a slave (cf. Lev 14:8 and Num 8:7), and one month was allowed to her for mourning (cf. Num 20:29; Deu 34:8). This humanitarian provision—unique in the ancient world —offered a period of adjustment from a former family relationship to the prospects of a new life in Israel. If the man, having married this captive, later decided on divorce for which provision was made (cf. 24:1-4 and Mt 19:8), he was not permitted to sell her back into slavery. She had the right of freedom (21:10-14).

The principle that a father's authority was not absolute in a home is illustrated by the example of the rights of a firstborn son (21:15-17). The oldest son had preferential inheritance rights and received a double portion of the family property equal to twice as much as each of the other sons. The father could not transfer this right to another son whom he might like better. This did not apply to sons of a concubine (Gen 21:9-13), or in cases of misconduct (Gen 49:3-4). Note that Jesus was called the firstborn (Col 1:18; Heb 1:6), a term which denoted preeminence as well as order of birth.

A father's right was enforced by the sanctions of theocratic law but not to the point of tyranny. If a son is rebellious toward his parents and refuses to listen to them, then they—both father and mother—may bring him to the elders of the city who are responsible to stone the defiant son. In this way parental responsibility was sustained by official judicial authority (21:18-21). Parents are God's representatives to their children.

Justice and righteousness have their source in God. The criminal's corpse was a public proclamation of the fact that justice was satisfied and that the curse of God had been embodied in his death. Consequently a criminal's body that embodied God's curse was to be buried before sunset in order to avert defilement of Israel's land (21:22-23). Paul reflects the content of this curse in his reference to the death of Christ (Gal 3:13). These verses also provide the background for the removal of Christ's body from the cross before sunset (Jn 19:31).

THE LAW OF LOVE APPLIED IN DOMESTIC AND SOCIAL RELATIONSHIPS (22:1—26:19)

Love for God—which was foremost and basic in the life of an Israelite—was to find a practical expression toward his fellowmen. Some of the ways in which love for one's neighbor was evident in daily life are delineated in this passage, 22:1—26:19. Included are some additional regulations for the family and the home and even instructions for the proper care of animals and fields. Although these precepts are given in a miscellaneous order—as is natural enough in a spoken discourse—we shall discuss them topically.

In delineating these instructions, Moses reminds the Israelites of the basis or background for reflecting this love toward their fellowmen. They are reminded that prosperity, righteousness, and blessings are for the people who exemplify and reflect a proper respect for their fellowmen.

Since love and respect for neighbors is related to God, the instructions concerning hatred and revenge must be recognized as component parts. Those who set themselves up against God and His people await the judgment of God.

FAMILY LIFE (22:13-30; 24:1-5; 25:5-12)

The establishment of a home was not to be interrupted during the first year by military service (24:5). This gave the newlyweds the opportunity to enjoy their matrimonial relationship. Note also other considerations favorable to family life in 20:5-8.

Conjugal rights were to be observed with proper respect for each other (22:13-30). If a man marries and subsequently brings charges against his wife claiming that she was not a virgin, then the charges must be heard before the city elders. If the husband is not sustained in his charge then he shall be punished by paying a fine which is given to his father-in-law, and the husband must retain her as his wife without the possibility of divorce. If the husband's charges are sustained, then the wife must be stoned in order to purge the evil from the community.

If a man cohabits with a married woman, then both are to be executed by stoning (22:22). If a betrothed girl is seduced, the guilty man is to be stoned, but the girl is only subject to execution if she was attacked in a city or a population center and did not cry for help. If such an attack occurred in a sparsely settled area the girl was not held responsible and therefore not subject to execution.

If an unbetrothed girl was seduced, then the guilty man was required to pay the required fee to her father and marry her without the right of divorce (22:23-29). In no case was a man allowed to marry his father's wife (22:30). By observing these regulations concerning marriage and divorce, the Israelites were to maintain and preserve the sanctity of family life and the home.

The Mosaic law under certain circumstances permitted divorce because of the hardheartedness of the Israelites (Mt 19:8 and Mk 10:5), but it was not mandatory. Priests were forbidden to marry divorced people (Lev 21:7, 14; and 22:13).

In Deuteronomy 24 the first three verses state the conditions and should be read as one sentence, while verse 4 states the conclusion. In case of adultery the death penalty was in order, as noted above in 22:13-30 (cf. Lev 20:10).

When a man for some reason, which is not clearly indicated in the text, seeks a divorce, he must provide a writ of separation which very likely was prepared by a public officer who decided the adequacy of the grounds of the divorce. This legal document was given to the woman for her protection. Subsequently they could not be remarried to each other if the woman in the meantime had married another man (cf. Jer 3:1). The verdict of declaring this woman as defiled for purposes of reuniting the original couple may have been intended to temper needless separation and divorce in breaking up a home.

Levirate (from Latin *levir,* "husband's brother") marriages provided that the brother of a deceased man who died childless was to marry the widow in order to provide an heir. These marriages were not compulsory in Israel, and here in Deuteronomy 25:5-10 the instructions apply to brothers who share the same estate. This was not contrary to the warnings given in Leviticus 18:16 and 20:21. Even though not compulsory, this practice reflected fraternal affection, and if anyone refused to conform to this practice, his refusal apparently demanded consideration by the elders. The perpetuation of his name as a member of the covenant seed witnessed to the dignity of the individual. Since Numbers 27:4-8 gave daughters the right of inheritance when there were no sons in a family, it is reasonable to read "no child" rather than "no son" in 25:5 (cf. Tamar, Gen 38:8-10, and the Boaz-Ruth marriage, Ru 4:1-17).

Slave traffic and man stealing were forbidden under penalty of death (24:7). The rights and dignity of the individual person were to be properly safeguarded and protected in the society of Israel. A person who had been enslaved and came among the Israelites for refuge was not to be returned to his former master, but given the opportunity to live in the place of his choice. He was not to be mistreated by the Israelites (23:15-16).

Matters of dress and apparel receive brief attention. The exchange of men's and women's garments (22:5), may reflect pagan practices which were not permissible for the Israelites at that time. Although the details are not known to us, the fact that this practice was abhorrent to Israel's God indicates that in their contemporary culture it violated the distinction God had made between man and woman.

Tassels were to be attached to their outer garments (22:12). These were to serve as constant reminders about their relationship with God (Num 15:37-41). This positive outward means of remembrance was designed to prevent them from being led into ways of sin and harlotry.

Laws of health pertaining to camp life were also emphasized (23:9-14). Cleanliness of body and clothes was to be observed with great care. Human excretions were to be buried properly. Even in modern times where this is not done or where the excretions are used for fertilizing potatoes or other produce, the health of the community is endangered. The Israelites even in war were to acknowledge God in their midst. Holiness was symbolized by physical cleanliness among God's covenant people.

When an Israelite built a house it was essential that he construct a parapet around the roof—if it was flat and accessible—lest anyone fall to the ground from the housetop (22:8). This represented practical concern for others.

COMPASSION AND JUSTICE (22:1-4, 24:5-22, 25:1-4)

In matters of food and sustenance the Israelites were to exercise great care toward their fellowmen. The mill or millstone could not be taken as security for payment of debt since they were indispensable for the preparation of daily food (24:6). If these were taken away, life itself would be threatened or endangered.

Wages were to be paid daily to the hired servant or to the immigrant to whom the daily wage was essential for his sustenance (24:14-15). In cases where the withholding of daily remuneration actually resulted in hardship and oppression, the Israelite was reminded that if he truly loved his neighbor he would be sensitive to his needs in terms of daily responsibility.

At harvesttime the owner was instructed to leave the gleanings in the vineyard as well as in his grainfield, so that the poor and needy could come and glean the remains (24:19-21). This provided opportunity for the immigrants, orphans, and widows to gather some food for their sustenance.

Any person entering his neighbor's vineyard was allowed to eat all he cared to eat. Or if he was walking through the field of grain he could eat all he cared to eat in order to satisfy his hunger. In either case, however, he was not permitted to take any grapes or grain with him (23:24-25). In this way, his immediate personal needs would be met, but at the same time the poor were not allowed to take advantage of the one who produced the crops.

The poor and needy were not to be exploited by those who were endowed with more material things. The practice of not charging interest for loans made to fellow Israelites (23:19-20), should be interpreted in the context of Exodus 22:25 and Leviticus 25:35-36 (cf. Deu 15:1-11). When an Israelite loaned to a poor and needy person, the lender should have a heart of compassion and neighborly love for the individual in need of the essentials of life.

Loans made to foreigners very likely were made for business purposes and therefore were subject to interest, but even a foreigner or an alien was not to be mistreated if payment created a serious hardship. If a man could not make his payment on a loan the collector had no right to take personal belongings such as his coat, which was essential for his covering at night (24:10-13). The Israelite was to show love and compassion since he himself had been the recipient of God's mercy when he was in Egyptian bondage.

In business dealings the Israelite was expected to use just weights and measures (25:13-16; cf. Lev 19:35-37). Mistreatment of fellowmen in this respect is an abomination unto God. God's righteousness is to be reflected in man's treatment of his fellowmen in everyday business affairs. The Israelite was to observe this because God had redeemed him out of Egypt.

The practice of justice seemed to have a daily application in the consideration that was given to the needs of widows, orphans, and immigrants. Mistreatment of these frequently served as an index to sins of society at large in the preaching of the prophets in subsequent centuries. The widow's dress, representing her personal essential necessity for life, was not to be taken as a pledge. If so, the creditor might be tempted to confiscate it in case payment was not made. The Israelite was never to forget that God had redeemed him from slavery (24:17-18). Having been the recipient of God's love and mercy in redemption, the Israelite out of this experience was to exercise love and compassion toward those who were less fortunate than he was. This was neighborly love put in practice in everyday life.

Personal responsibility was clearly delineated by Moses (24:16). Fathers were not to be executed for their sons nor sons for their fathers. Hate and revenge could not be gratified at the pleasure of the offended but must always be regulated by judges in the court (25:1-3).

The ox and the ass were not to be yoked together (22:10). This may have been for humanitarian reasons, since the step and pull of these animals are so unlike. In the classification of animals the ox is listed as a clean animal that could be used for an acceptable sacrifice. The ass, on the other hand, was an unclean animal requiring redemption by the sacrifice of a lamb. The observance of this law made them conscious of the fact that they were serving a holy God. When the ox was used for threshing grain, the ox should not be muzzled so that he could freely eat as much as he needed while rendering this service (25:4).

This regulation concerning the treatment of animals does not by any means cover all the questions that might be pending in the possession of animals, but it does give an index as to what the attitude of the owner should be. Man, in having control of the animals, should not needlessly exploit them but constantly treat them with fair consideration.

Various seeds were not to be sown in the same field, nor were garments to be made of mixed threads (22:9 and 11 cf. Lev 19:19). However, tassels and fringes of twisted threads were to be attached to their garments as visible reminders that they were obeying and serving God and not primarily concerned about their own selfish interests (22:12 cf. Num 15:37-41). The significance of these prohibitions in the light of Israel's contemporary culture may not be apparent to us today because of our lack of knowledge concerning the customs that prevailed at that time. Perhaps they were under temporary consideration for Israel's settlement in Canaan.

Brotherly love should find expression in regard to straying animals (22:1-4). Lost property in this case should be treated by the Israelite as he would treat his own. In consideration for the one who lost the property, the finder was under obligation to assume responsibility in returning it. In this way, the Israelite was instructed to exercise fair treatment toward his neighbor as well as the animal that had gone astray.

Instructions were also given concerning birds and their hatching habits (22:6-7 cf. Lev 22:28 and Ex 23:19). If an Israelite took the young birds from a nest, he was under obligation to let the mother bird go free. In this way a man could not take advantage of a mother bird, catching it while following her native instinct to remain with the young in the nest. Observance of this law in nature offered the observer the promise of long life and providential care.

THE CONGREGATION OF ISRAEL (23:1-25)

As a corporate body the Israelites had certain regulations as God's holy people. The exclusion of eunuchs (23:1-2) in the beginning of Israel's history may have had significance in the light of contemporary practices. Israelites were not to practice mutilation of the body (14:1), as other nations did. Note also the punishment for multilation of reproductive organs in 25:11-12.

Misuse of the body in prostitution was explicitly forbidden. The money accumulated by male (also called "dogs," cf. Rev 22:15) or female prostitutes was regarded as abhorrent to the God of Israel (23:17-18). The Canaanites practiced misuse of the body in their sacred rites of prostitution and child sacrifice and thereby precipitated their destruction. Hypocritical piety of bringing offerings to God, which they had obtained by misuse of the body, could not be tolerated. The body of man was more than any offering or gift man could bring. The giver was more important than the gift he might bring.

An offering might be brought in payment for a vow. Vows, however, were not mandatory, but once a person had made a vow, he was expected to keep it, out of reverance for God (23:21-23). (Concerning the details of a Nazarite vow see Num 6:1-21).

The sacredness of Israel in their relationship to surrounding nations is uniquely delineated through Moses. The Moabites and Ammonites—though not dispossessed of their land by the Israelites (2:9, 19)—were excluded from participation in the Israelite congregation because of their endeavor to bring a divine curse upon God's chosen people (23:3-6) instead of offering them hospitality. God's love for Israel had been manifested in a peculiar way in turning the intended curse into a blessing when Balaam had been hired by Balak the Moabite king (cf. Num 22-24). The Egyptians and Edomites, however, were accorded more favorable acceptance among the Israelites who once had been strangers themselves (23:7-8).

PROMISES AND WARNINGS (22:5-12; 25:13-19)

Throughout these extended instructions and admonitions in which the Israelites are encouraged to constantly express their wholehearted devotion to God in their daily lives, there are also the promises and assurances of God's continued goodness and mercy as well as warnings. In this manner a vital relationship with God was not only initially established, but it could also be maintained. These promises undoubtedly were designed to provide a stimulant in their total pattern of living.

Proper and generous treatment of the destitute and

needy would not only evoke words of blessings from the recipients but would also be reckoned by God as righteousness (24:13). Works of doing good to those in need were acceptable to God when performed by one who was in a love relationship with God.

Enjoyment of life was promised to the one who carefully regarded the laws concerning the treatment of birds (22:6-7).

Solemn was the warning, however, issued about mistreating the poor. Mistreatment of fellowmen reflected a lack of proper respect and reverence for God. Withholding daily wages from the needy might result in a poor man's appeal to God for help so that a divine rebuke was pending (24:15). Shortchanging the poor and needy by weights and measures was an abomination to the God whom the Israelites served 25:15-16. This represented a warning of great magnitude, since the one who ignored or mistreated the poor would be accountable to God for his neglect.

The most impressive warning seems to be the reminder of the incident which precipitated Miriam's leprosy (24:8-9 cf. Num 12:10-15). If Miriam, the sister of Moses through whom God revealed Himself to Israel, was smitten with leprosy for her murmuring and rebellion, how much more should the average Israelite take care lest he transgress and be smitten by such a deadly disease in divine judgment?

Repeatedly they were reminded that they had come out of Egyptian bondage (24:18, 22). This historical fact should always temper them in any consideration of mistreating their fellowmen. They had been the recipients of God's mercy; therefore they were to exercise mercy toward their fellowmen. Their love for God was to be wholehearted and without reservation. Their love for their neighbors was to be regulated by the God who exercises love and righteousness.*

ISRAEL'S CONFESSION IN WORSHIP (26:1-19)

Having delineated the rights and obligations of his people in their divine relationship, Moses instructs the Israelites in the liturgies of two confessions and a reaffirmation of the covenant. In this manner they are to acknowledge and worship God after they have occupied the land of promise (26:1-19). Through these confessions, acts of dedication, and worship, they are to maintain a continued consciousness of God as their redeemer and sustainer and impart this to each successive generation. What a beautiful model of prayer and praise for God-fearing people in every generation.

The occasion for the first confession (26:1-11) is the offering of the firstfruits (cf. Ex 23:19; 34:26; Num 18:12-17). The offering of firstfruits occurred frequently throughout the year. This constituted a part of the annual festivals as noted in Deuteronomy 16. A sheaf of firstfruits was waved at the Feast of Unleavened Bread following the Passover (Lev 23:10). The Feast of Weeks was called "the day of firstfruits" (Num 28:26). On this occasion two loaves were offered (Lev 23:17). Since the grape harvest was late in the year, the firstfruits of the vine could not be offered until the celebration of the Feast of Tabernacles. Possibly it was the presentation of the firstfruits of the vine at the Feast of Tabernacles that Moses had in mind in this confession of the Israelites as they appeared at the central place of worship.

*Meredith Kline expresses this pointedly. "Taken together, the laws of love and hate amount to the single requirement to love God, and expressive of this love of God, to love whom he loves and hate whom he hates" (*Wycliffe Bible Commentary*, p. 189).

When the offerer presented his basket of firstfruits to the priest, he verbally acknowledged that he was now living in the land which God had promised to his fathers (26:3). Following this, the priest placed the basket before the altar of the Lord.

The confession that follows (26:5-10) begins with a reference to Jacob as a "wandering Aramean" (RSV). When Jacob fled from his home in Beersheba he passed through Syria (Aram) to Mesopotamia (Aram Naharaiim, Gen 24:10, Jer. Bible) to live with Laban his uncle. Returning from there, Jacob was overtaken by Laban after he came through Syria at the Jabbok River where he not only faced the wrath of Laban but also that of Esau his brother. Later, the famine in Canaan necessitated his migration to Egypt. When the Israelites became populous and powerful, they were oppressed by the Egyptians, but it was God who responded to their prayers and miraculously delivered them out of Egypt. It was God who enabled them to enter and conquer the land from which firstfruits were now presented before the altar.

The essential aspects of the worshiper's coming to the sanctuary were the presentation of the firstfruits, bowing in worship, and rejoicing in the Lord's goodness. In this manner the visit to the sanctuary was a confession and acknowledgment of God. It was a time of praise and rejoicing because of God's goodness and mercy extended to former generations and evidence of divine sustaining grace at that time.

The second confession (26:12-15) is related to the giving of the tithe every third year to the poor and needy in their community (cf. 14:28-29). This tithe was not brought to the central sanctuary but distributed to the Levite, the immigrant, the orphan, and the widow in their local communities. In this manner the Israelite expressed in a material way his love and concern for his neighbor. After he had done this according to the instructions, then he would come and make his confession before God. This was at the end of the harvest season, probably at the observance of the Feast of Tabernacles, when all the tithe had been accounted for after the harvest.

In this confession the Israelite acknowledges publicly before God that he has actually shared with his fellow citizens the tithe of his income according to the divine instructions. Defilement, uncleanness, and offerings to the dead—these practices and others that prevailed in their contemporary pagan cultures—he had carefully avoided (cf. Lev 22:3 and Num 19:11). Confessing that he had acted in obedience to God's voice, he prayerfully petitioned God to bless his people and the land (ground) which God had given them in fulfillment of his oath to their forefathers (26:13-15). In this manner the Israelite confessed his continual dependence upon the Lord his God and lived in the expectancy of God's continued blessing.

The Israelites had ratified their covenant with God at Sinai (Ex 24:7). Here on the Plains of Moab, Moses had plainly declared the stipulations or requirements of the covenant renewal between the Israelites and their God (Deu 5-25). In accepting the terms of this agreement—acknowledging that the Lord is their God, promising wholehearted obedience, and an attitude of listening to God's voice—the Israelites were assured that they were His people and that they would be the foremost of all nations (26:16-19).

4

ALTERNATIVES FOR A
GOD-RELATED PEOPLE

(27:1—30:20)

CURSES AND BLESSINGS normally constituted an essential part of the Near Eastern suzerainty treaties during the latter half of the second millennium B.C. When Moses addressed Israel on the Plains of Moab, in delineating their responsibilities to maintain their obligations as God's covenant people, he very succinctly faced them with the alternatives of the divine blessings and curses (27:1—30:20).

These chapters also contain instructions for the renewal of their covenant treaty under Joshua and the personal admonition of Moses. In 26:16-19 Moses points to their public declaration to serve God. In this public ceremony under Moses, chapter 28 may have followed chapter 26, chapter 30 may have followed chapter 28, and finally in its written literary form chapters 27 and 29 may have been inserted.

Taken as a whole, this passage provides for the ratification of the law both under Moses before his death and under Joshua as he took office. Moses served as the great mediator between the Israelites and their God. Joshua by divine appointment was the successor to Moses in this ministry under the suzerainty of God. In contemporary secular situations it was customary for a king before his death to secure from a vassal the pledge of allegiance to himself and his son and then arrange that subsequent to his death this renewal pledge be repeated to his son who succeeded him as ruler.

COVENANT RENEWAL UNDER JOSHUA (27:1-26)

Instructions for the renewal of the covenant were given by Moses and supported by the elders and priests. The preparations for this public ceremony were twofold. First, stones were to be erected, on which portions of the law were copied and made publicly available for the Israelites to read. Second, an altar was to be erected for the purpose of offering sacrifices. Mount Ebal is the place where the altar and the stones for recording the law were to be erected. It was in this setting that the curses were to be read publicly to all Israel.

THE PREPARATION FOR RENEWAL (27:1-14)

The basic stipulations of the Sinaitic covenant had been inscribed on tablets of stone, but upon arrival in the land of promise, the Israelites were to erect large stone pillars. Following the method known in Egypt, they were to cover these stones with plaster and then inscribe the words of the covenantal agreement. These inscribed stones offered constant witness to their relationship with God, making it known publicly to everyone (cf. 31:26; Jos 24:26-27). In this manner, provision was made for coming generations to read for themselves the agreement that existed between the Israelites and their God.

The altar was to be erected at the foot of Mount Ebal,

near the great stones containing the law. Unhewn stone was to be used for this altar, as had been the case at Mount Sinai where God revealed Himself to Israel (Ex 20:25). In contemporary culture, heathen altars were hewn out of a rock outcropping or built of cut stones and adorned with idols. The Israelites were not to conform to these idolatrous ways, but were to recognize the altar as a place of God's revelation where the human and divine met.

Mount Ebal, where the altar and great stones inscribed with the law were erected, was the place where the curses were to be read publicly. Over against Mount Ebal southward was Mount Gerizim with the city of Shechem nearby in the valley. Whereas the blessings were to be hailed from the latter mountain, the curses were to be proclaimed to those on Mount Ebal, where a natural concavity in the hillside forms a huge outdoor theater. In the valley between the two groups of tribes arrayed opposite each other were placed the altar and the huge stones with the recorded Deuteronomic covenant.

Sacrifices were to be offered on the altar of God made from undressed stones. Burnt offerings and peace offerings were to be offered here, even as Israel had done when the covenantal relationship had been established at Mount Sinai (Ex 24:1-8). The burnt offerings which were completely consumed on the altar represented Israel's unreserved dedication to God. The peace offerings which expressed thanksgiving to God for health, salvation, or deliverance already granted were occasions of rejoicing. In this offering, the entire family and other invited guests shared in the meal prepared from part of the sacrifice.

This peace offering at Mount Ebal was a very significant and historic occasion, being the first in the promised land. It was here that Abram had erected his first altar in Canaan (Gen 12:6-7). The fact that this location was in the center of the land of Canaan also should make them aware of the fact that they actually were in possession of the land of promise.

The ceremonial feast was usually a part of the ratification activities when suzerainty treaties were signed in countries neighboring Israel during the Mosaic era. Consequently, the festal ceremonies associated with the joyous meal when burnt offerings were presented provided a proper setting at Mount Ebal for the renewal or reaffirmation of the covenant. Dedication, total commitment, thanksgiving, and rejoicing—these expressions were to characterize the Israelites as they assembled on Mount Ebal in the land of Canaan under Joshua.

The tribes of Israel were divided into two groups for the public reading of the curses and blessings in Canaan according to the instructions given in chapter 27. The details are not delineated, and in 27:15-26 only the self-maledictions are given. Very likely the six blessings (28:3-6) and the six curses (28:16-19) are involved, according to 27:12-13. The actual arrangement probably provided that the priests stood by the ark of the covenant between the two mountains, with six tribes located northward toward or on Mount Ebal, and six tribes southward toward or on Mount Gerizim. The priests and Levites read or pronounced the blessings and curses with the people responding the "Amen" of confirmation.

The division into two tribal groups was as follows. Six of the tribes descending from Jacob's wives Leah and Rachel—Simeon, Levi, Judah, Issachar, Joseph, and Benjamin—were assembled on the slopes of Mount Gerizim responding to the blessings; the remaining tribes—Gad, Asher, Dan, and Naphtali were the descendants of the sons of the handmaids of Leah and Rachel, and the tribe of Zebulon, the youngest son of Leah; and the tribe of

Reuben, who forfeited the birthright by the sin of incest (Gen 49:4; cf. Deu 27:20)—were assembled on the slopes of Ebal responding to the curses.

Although details are not given, it does not seem reasonable that the tribes on Mount Ebal were cursed or that the tribes on Mount Gerizim were particularly blessed. Each group reponded with an "Amen" confirming for the entire nation that the conditions of the blessing or curse would prevail in accordance with their obedience or transgression of the covenant agreement. Could it be that the curses were directed toward Mount Ebal where the copy of the Deuteronomic covenant and the altar were visible? If so, this would avoid any inference that the curses had any particular application to the tribes giving the actual verbal confirmation of judgment in case of disobedience. Within the hearing distance of the curses was the availability of the altar, signifying God's place of revelation to man. The curse as well as the blessing were under the control of God and came to man through God's direction, depending on man's concern to obey God.

Within the context of these instructions intended for living in Canaan, 27:1-7, Moses together with the priests reminds the people assembled before him on the Plains of Moab that on the very day when Moses is giving these instructions, they are openly confessing that they are God's people (27:9-10).

THE SELF-MALEDICTION (27:15-26)

The actual oath in ancient covenant ceremonies usually consisted of provisional self-malediction. Benedictions were not normally included in such an oath. With this proclamation of twelve self-maledictions the priests led Israel in the oath of ratification of the covenant. As the expression "cursed be" was repeated again and again, the Israelites were reminded that as covenant breakers they were subjected to the same fate as the serpent and the ground were when Adam and Eve forfeited their relationship with God in the Garden of Eden.

The twelve crimes listed here as basically significant may be classified as follows:

1. The sins of idolatry, verse 15
2. Sins against fellowmen, verses 16-19
3. Sexual sins, verses 20-23
4. Guilt in bloodshed, verses 24-25
5. Concluding curse, verse 26.

The greatest and most common offense to mar Israel's relationship with God was idolatry. The lack of any graven image or likeness of God made by man uniquely distinguished them from the surrounding nations in their contemporary culture. Exclusive devotion to God could under no circumstances include any toleration or recognition of other gods. Consequently, it is not surprising to find this curse at the head of the list. Israel's God was not the creative product of man's imagination, but Israel's God had created man and the universe. Consequently, there was not any allowance for tolerance or compromise as far as idolatry was concerned.

The next four curses affect man's relationship with his fellowmen. First and foremost in duty to fellowmen is man's duty toward his parents. Normally an individual becomes aware of his relationship with his parents first. The individual who recognizes that they provided shelter, food, protection, education, and other benefits in life is obligated under God (Ex 20:12) to honor, revere, and obey his parents.

In Egypt, filial piety was taught to the growing child, and a disobedient son forfeited prospects of happiness in

the future. Confucianism required the most complete sub-
jection to parental authority. Subsequently in Greek culture
Aristotle taught that the relation of children to their parents
was parallel to that of men to God. In Rome the entire
state system was based on the absolute authority of the
father. Although a curse is pronounced upon the Israelite
who dishonors his parents, the details of the basic principle
of honoring parents are not delineated. Within the total
pattern of behavior that reflected the proper love and respect for God was included the proper love and respect
for parents. To dishonor or mistreat parents while pro-
fessing to maintain a vital relationship with God is to
dishonor God.

The rights of neighbors are to be regarded with justice.
A curse rests upon the one who enlarges his property by
moving his neighbor's landmark. God expects man to be
fair to his neighbor, because God has created him and
loves him. Proper respect for God must find a practical
expression in the practical matters in daily life in relationship with neighbors. A holy and righteous God does not
tolerate injustice. Neither should anyone who professes to
love God wholeheartedly.

The man who takes advantage of the blind by misleading
them, or the man who mistreats the immigrant, the widow,
and the fatherless, is also divinely cursed. From the human
perspective these people may have been overtaken by the
misfortunes of life. Those who are more favorably situated
and blessed are to reflect God's love and consideration for
these people in sharing, aiding, and helping them, instead
of taking advantage of them in times of adverse circumstances.

Four curses are directed toward individuals who might
be guilty of incest or sexual sins in disrupting family life.
The purity and proper use of sex must be safeguarded

among God's people. Misuse of sex in family life as well as perverted sexual relations with animals are forbidden and subject to God's curse (27:20-23 cf. Lev 18:8-9, 17, 23).

Life itself was a sacred trust (27:24-25). Divinely cursed was any one who was guilty of secret or judicial murder (cf. Ex 20:13, 23:7; Num 35:16).

The final, concluding imprecation is directed toward the one who fails to make the laws or directives for living as God's people the model and pattern of his life and conduct. Since this last curse is all-inclusive, it seems reasonable to conclude that the preceding curses represent various sins selected by way of example. Most of these were sins that could easily be concealed from judicial authorities, but the divine curses pronounced here made the populace of Israel aware anew of the fact that they were accountable to God, from whose presence no sin could be hidden. Their relationship was primarily and ultimately with God. Love for God was the basis, and out of this vital relationship should normally issue a right relationship toward fellowmen.

THE TWO WAYS (28:1-68)

In this chapter Moses sets before the Israelites the way of blessing and the way of cursing. In his responsibility as leader and mediator, Moses had previously conveyed to the Israelites, when the covenant was established at Mount Sinai, the promise of God's blessing and the warning that they should not turn to other gods (Ex 23:20-33). After their rebellion against the Sinaitic covenant, Moses warned them (Lev 26) of the divine judgment that would overtake them if they disobeyed.

After thirty-eight years of wilderness wanderings, Moses presents to this new generation in simple and appealing language the alternatives of God's mercies and God's curses, depending on their response. The blessings of God which the Israelites had already experienced under Moses' leadership are outlined briefly (28:1-14), while the consequences of disobedience are delineated more extensively (28:15-68). The latter are portrayed in a series of prophetic pictures in which the disastrous results for Israel are vividly set forth.

GOD'S FAVOR (28:1-14)

Israel did not legally merit the goodness of God which was bestowed upon them, but at the same time their concern to maintain a right relationship with God was essential for their continual well-being as a nation in the land which God provided for them. God's favor is summarily expressed in the following beatitudes:

> Blessed shall you be in the city;
> Blessed shall you be in the field.
> Blessed shall be the
> > fruit of your body,
> > fruit of your soul,
> > fruit of your livestock,
> > increase of your herds,
> > young of your flocks;
> Blessed shall be your baskets
> > and your kneading trough.
> Blessed shall you be when you come in;
> Blessed shall you be when you go out.

These beatitudes are pointed and comprehensive. The blessings of God will rest upon them in the city as well as in the field. Fruitfulness of the family, livestock, the field, and every endeavor will be their providential lot in their whole pattern of living. These divine favors will overtake them if they will be consistently concerned about living in obedience to that which God has revealed to them.

That God's favor and blessing are intended to permeate the totality of all their endeavors is emphasized again in an expanded summary in 28:7-14. God promised to grant them victory over their enemies. God promised to give them possession of the land of Canaan. God promised to make them successful in all their activities so that their land would be productive. God promised to establish them as a people dedicated to Himself

> If they would
> > keep the commandments of the Lord
> > > > > > and
> > walk in His ways,
> When they obey the commandment of God,
> > not deviating to the right or to the left,
> > not turning toward idols to worship them;
> Then God will
> > make Israel the head and not the tail,
> > prosper them materially,
> > provide them with rain for their crops,
> enrich them so they can lend to many nations,
> grant them recognition as God's people by all the
> > > > > nations of the earth.

In this manner Moses outlined the comprehensiveness of God's blessing for the generation of Israelites who were anticipating the conquest and occupation of the land of promise.

THE WARNINGS CONCERNING GOD'S DISFAVOR (28:15-68)

Since the beatitudes were conditional so that the divine blessings had a direct relationship to their dedication and obedience, Moses also in a succinct manner announces the curses that will overtake them if they fail to pay attention to God and His instructions (28:15-19). Note how these parallel the beatitudes.

> Cursed shall you be in the city;
> Cursed shall you be in the field.
> Cursed shall be your basket
>   and your kneading trough;
> Cursed shall be the
>   fruit of your body,
>   produce of your soil,
>   offspring of your cattle,
>   young of your flock.
> Cursed shall you be when you come in;
> Cursed shall you be when you go out.

On the basis of his experience Moses was keenly aware of the fact that the Israelites were apt to be unfaithful in their allegiance to God. The extreme malediction for Israel was the possibility of being banished from the land of promise into the exilic bondage under pagan rulers. The loss of their identity as God's people and their place of worship in the land of promise represent the curse of God bringing upon Israel its greatest calamity. Consequently Moses portrays in extended warnings the disastrous results that will come if they disobey.

Forsaking God, or a diminishing of their wholehearted love and devotion toward God, is the sin that will precipitate God's curse upon them (29:20-28). Every endeavor will fail when God sends His curse instead of His blessing, so that they will be destroyed through pestilence and drought. The heavens will be brass and the earth will be iron when God withholds the rain. They will be defeated by their enemies so that they will become a horrible spectacle to all the kingdoms of the earth. The birds of the air will prey on their corpses without interference.

In 29:27-37 Moses delineates the details of the terrifying

conditions for the survivors that will be taken into exile. The boils of Egypt, ulcer, scurvy, incurable itch — these will affect them physically without any prospects of relief or healing. Madness, blindness, and confusion of mind will prevail so that the Israelites will be robbed and oppressed by invaders who will abuse the women, and confiscate their crops and livestock. Finally the Israelites with their sons, daughters, and their king will be taken into exile by a foreign nation. There they will serve gods of wood and stone. There they will become a byword or object of horror among the nations.

In 29:38-46 Moses portrays the pathos of the Israelites as the curse of exile overtakes them. In their effort to raise crops and produce their food supply, they will be frustrated as worms destroy their vineyards and locusts consume their trees as well as their crops. Sons and daughters born to them will be taken into exile. The alien and stranger in the land will prosper materially and provide loans to the Israelites. The former will be the head and the latter will be the tail. This disintegration and destruction of the Israelites will come when the Israelites refuse to listen to the voice of God. The breakdown of their vital relationship of love and obedience Godward will gradually result in the withdrawal of God's blessings and the release of God's curse upon them. These curses will come upon the Israelites for a sign and a wonder, exciting astonishment and terror because they had failed in their obligation to God.

The terrible conditions of this siege and ultimate capitulation to the invaders is most vividly portrayed by Moses in 29:47-57. The tragic scene of starvation, immorality, and revolting conditions prevailing during the time of this siege is graphically described against the background of Israel's lack of appreciation of God's goodness. Under God's blessing the Israelites were to serve the Lord with joyfulness and gladness of heart. Because of the fact that they did not appreciate God's goodness sufficiently to express their thankfulness in joyful living and praise, God would bring upon them a nation whose speech they did not understand. Since the Israelites did not appreciate God's mercy, they would be subjected to a people of fierce countenance descending upon them like a vulture, showing neither regard for the old nor mercy to the young. Because the Israelites put their trust in fortified walls instead of maintaining a continual confidence in God, their cities would be besieged successfully. Famine conditions would be so intense that the Israelites would eat the flesh of their own sons and daughters. Women would even eat the afterbirth of their wombs because of the terrible famine. The severity and extent of the siege and prevailing hunger imposed upon Israel by the invading enemies is Israel's lot, because they failed to rejoice in the mercies of God and put their trust in the fortified walls they had built.

Beginning with the termination of the Northern Kingdom in 722 B.C., earlier conditions spoken of by Moses repeatedly overtook God's chosen people. The greatest judgment in Old Testament times in Israelite history took its toll in 586 B.C., when the glorious temple of Solomon and the city of Jerusalem, the capital of Davidic fame, were reduced to ashes and abandoned. Although the Jews returned from Babylonian captivity to rebuild Jerusalem, they were subjected to a greater and more tragic exile in A.D. 70. According to the vivid description by Josephus, Jews were slaughtered by the thousands when the Roman army of Titus mercilessly suppressed the Jewish revolt and destroyed Jerusalem. Ironically Jews were taken as slaves to Egypt and other parts of the world. Not until 1948 did the Jews reestablish their own commonwealth and revive Hebrew as a living language. Even today the golden-domed

Muslim edifice, erected during the seventh century A.D., stands on the site where the temple once stood.

In the concluding verses (28:58-68), Moses makes a direct comparison between the past and the future. The plagues of Egypt, which were so familiar to Moses from his own experience, had been primarily directed against Pharaoh and the Egyptians while Israel had been miraculously delivered from slavery. Because of this deliverance, the Israelites were to revere, love, and honor God. If the future generations failed to revere the glorious and awesome name of God, then the diseases of Egypt would be divinely released upon the Israelites so that they would be dislodged from their promised land and scattered from one end of the earth to the other. There they would serve gods of wood and stone unknown to the Israelites. In exile they would live in fear and insecurity, so that the weariness of soul would cause them to dread the dawn of each new day. Ultimately, they will be brought back to Egypt where they will be offered as slaves to the enemies, but no one will even want to buy the Israelites as slaves.

From his Egyptian background and experience, Moses must have reflected on the oppression and enslavement of his own people as he portrayed to the new generation the conditions that would result from their disregard for the God who had redeemed them out of Egyptian slavery. His concern was that they might so live that the divine beatitudes would be their lot.

THE COVENANT OATH (29:1-29)

PERSPECTIVE OF HISTORY (29:1-9)

The covenant between God and Israel which had been established under Moses at Mt. Horeb was now renewed with this new generation in Moab. The words in 29:1

might fittingly describe the preceding chapter as well as
the rest of this chapter, where Moses makes a direct personal appeal.

In a forthright manner Moses reminds the Israelites
that they had witnessed and experienced what God had
done for them during their wilderness experience (29:2-
9). Yet they did not fully appreciate or comprehend the
significance of God's supernatural providence. The clothes
of the Israelites had not worn out, nor had they labored
for their food supply, which was so bountifully provided
for them throughout the forty years of wilderness wanderings. The kings east of the river Jordan—Sihon, king of
Heshbon, and Og, the king of Bashan—had been defeated,
yielding their territory to the Reubenites, Gadites, and half
of the tribe of Manasseh. All of this happened that they
might "know" or "realize" in an experiential way that "I
am the LORD your God" (29:6). A full realization that
God was the one who gave them the ability to gain release
from Egypt and to come to the threshhold of the land of
Canaan conveyed to them what God was like. God's interest, love, and concern for Israel had been daily evident
in the everyday experiences of the Israelites under the
leadership of Moses.

THE RIGHT WAY (29:10-15)

As Moses speaks to them, they are reminded that they
are standing before God. The solemnity of this covenant
is vividly impressed upon them. The entire community—
men, women, children, non-Israelites, and servants—is
present for this public ratification. The people of Israel
were entering into a covenant even as Abram (Gen 17) and
the generation of Israelites that had died in the wilderness
(Ex 20-24) had done before them. This covenantal relationship did not represent a conquest by a superior power

or the humiliating subjugation of the people—as usually was the case in contemporary suzerainty treaties between the conqueror and the conquered—but displayed God's redemptive grace in which God fulfilled His promise made previously to the patriarchs, Abraham, Isaac, and Jacob. This relationship between God and the Israelites was not only intended for those entering into this covenant under Moses but also for generations to follow. Note that Jesus included the generations to follow in His prayer of intercession, John 17:20-21.

The sublimity of this relationship should not be overlooked. God provided all this that the Israelites might be established as a people devoted to God and that God might be known as the God of Israel (29:13).

THE WARNINGS (29:16-29)

Once more, the contrast is vividly drawn between the Israelites and their God and the pagan nations and their gods. In their experience the Israelites had seen that the idols of Egypt and gods of other nations, through whose territory they had passed, were gods made of wood, stone, silver, and gold. How foolish for the Israelites to consider turning away from their God. How foolish to turn to man-made idols.

The destructive fruit of idolatry is like a poisonous plant. Idolatry precipitates God's curse and wrath. If idolatry were permitted to permeate Israel, it would mean ruin and death. The individual who turned to idolatry could not assume that he could hide his idolatry among God's covenant people. God's curse would certainly be invoked upon him.

What tragic consequences God's judgment would bring could easily be visualized by Moses and his people as Moses addressed them on the Plains of Moab. Looking

westward the Israelites could see the borders of the Dead
Sea which stretched out before them a distance of forty-
six miles from north to south. Appropriately known as
the "Salt Sea" it offered witness to the terrible desolation
which in times past had come upon the vale of Siddim
which once resembled paradise but had been destroyed
under God's judgment (Gen 13:10 and 19:24).

The modern tourist standing on the western edge of the
Dead Sea near its southern end can see a huge sign on
which the following is recorded:

> And the LORD rained upon Sodom and upon Gomorrah
> brimstone and fire from the LORD out of heaven;
> And he overthrew those cities, and all the plain, and
> all the inhabitants of the cities, and that which grew upon
> the ground (Genesis 19:24-25).

The barrenness and desolation around the Dead Sea at
almost thirteen hundred feet below sea level gave witness
to the Israelites (as well as to the modern tourist) to the
devastating effects of God's judgment upon a valley that
was known for its fertility when Lot was attracted to this
productive area.

Moses warned his people that turning to idolatry would
be similar to roots producing poison and wormwood,
bringing God's destructive judgment. When foreigners
would see the land of the Israelites as desolate as the plains
of Sodom and Gomorrah they would be told that this was
caused by Israel's disobedience in breaking the covenant
and turning to idolatry. Even as the barren waste surrounding the Dead Sea served as a reminder of God's wrath
upon the wicked cities of Sodom and Gomorrah, so the
desolation of Canaan would be evidence of God's wrath
upon the Israelites who had turned to idolatry.

The expression of pious submission and a solemn

admonition in 29:29 provide a fitting conclusion to the covenantal terms given through Moses. Man is limited in his knowledge and should constantly be aware of the fact that there is much that is unknown to him but known to God. What God has revealed was sufficient for that generation and for those who followed. Man is responsible to respond in love and obedience to God according to that which God has revealed. This was the design and purpose of God's revelation to them. Moses was concerned that the new generation of Israelites would take advantage of this opportunity and responsibility. In this way they would realize God's goodness for them.

RESTORATION HOPES (30:1-10)

God's message through Moses included a basis for faith and hope for those who had a right attitude toward God. Moses did not conclude with a hopeless warning of desolation and destruction that would come as a result of invoking God's curse through disobedience. Divine assurance is given through Moses that they would have the opportunity of returning from captivity.

The cause of dispersion would be a lack of love for God which was evident in their failure to conform to the written requirements which God expected of them as His holy people. The basic problem was not legalism or an outward pattern of observing all the meticulous details of the law. The heart, which was the center of the will, needed to be circumcised (30:6 and 10:16). Moses was not speaking of the outward act of circumcision but of a spiritual circumcision of the heart, a cutting away of selfish ambition and stubbornness which caused spiritual insensitivity and lack of devotion (cf. Jer 4:4; Ro 2:28-29). This was a matter of a spiritual relationship with God in which both the human and divine dimensions were involved. Since the breaking of this relationship precipitated the invocation of God's curse, bringing about their exile, the reestablishment of this relationship was vital for restoration.

This promise is definite and conditional. Note the twofold aspect of this promise of restoration. God promised to give them a circumcised heart so that they would want to love Him. On the other hand, the Israelites have the responsibility to turn to God in repentance with all their hearts in full obedience. As a result, the divine curses resting upon Israel will be turned toward their enemies while the Israelites will experience the blessings of restoration.

In this way the prospects of God's curse and God's blessings are projected before the people of Israel. The prediction of captivity and dispersion because of their idolatry is tempered by the promise of ultimate restoration. Even though the nation might be subjected to God's curse, there was always the hope that they might be restored. For the God-fearing person this provided the basis for his faith and hope.

THE CRUCIAL DECISION (30:11-20)

The appeal of Moses to the new generation reaches its climax in these ten verses. Beyond all that Moses had done and can do the Israelites standing before Moses must make their decision. The future rests with them. Moses cannot make this decision for them. God in His providence has made conditions such that—within limits—man has the freedom of choice. In the final analysis, this choice is the responsibility of the individual.

Moses had solemnly warned them about the decisions the previous generation of Israelites had made when they failed to place their trust in God. After appraising the failures of the past and the prospects for the future, Moses earnestly admonished them to make the right choice. He made them keenly aware of the fact that God had chosen them, endowed them with life, freed them from slavery, brought them to the borders of Canaan, and promised them divine aid in the conquest and occupation of the land of promise, but the decision concerning their relationship with God *they* must make.

The key issue facing them in this decision is to love God so wholeheartedly that they will live in accordance with God's revealed will as outlined in His written revelation. Briefly and succinctly stated: it is the law of love.

This decision is very simple and yet profound. It was stated in simple terms so that they could understand and grasp what God expected of them. "It is not hidden from thee, neither is it far off" (30:11). It is not so marvelous or wonderful that they could not understand it. Although God had spoken from heaven, He had revealed Himself through Moses in words man could understand. Although they might think of God as being way out there in the heavens they also knew that this God had spoken through Moses in words simple enough for the Israelites to understand in their hearts and minds (30:14). (Note the suggestion in the Jerusalem Bible that verse 14 may refer to the concept of the Word of God further developed in Pr 8:22-23; Jn 1:1; Ro 10:6-8.) Neither were they to search at some distant point beyond the sea. All the information necessary for man to make his decision had been made known in language the Israelites could understand and grasp so that they could intelligently make their decision.

Moses pinpoints the matter. Basic to all else that any Israelite could do was the simple fact that he should love God. Without this, nothing else mattered. Love for neighbor, sacrifice, justice, social implications of the gospel—none of these is mentioned here. The starting point for implementing any of these in Israel's relationship to God is an all-out love for God. This is crucial, since all other efforts in serving God can only be realized in a manner pleasing to Him by beginning with a relationship of exclusive love and devotion Godward.

This decision to love or not to love God is one of life's major decisions. It is a decision the Israelites must make. It is a choice of life or death, of good or evil. They stand at the crossroads. One road leads to prosperity and salvation, while the other leads to adversity and destruction.

Moses cannot make this decision for them. They are responsible to respond for themselves and take the consequences of their choice. No additional research or change of circumstances is necessary but they must make up their minds. The crucial point is in their will. They must decide.

Moses calls heaven and earth to witness the fact that the Israelites are now confronted with this decision. Heaven and earth had witnessed that Moses had communicated to this generation of Israelites the knowledge of God's requirements. The resources of heaven, representing the divine, and earth, representing the human, have nothing more to offer as witnesses. This is the ultimate in this transaction between God and man.

If they choose to love God, then they will enjoy the blessings God has provided for them in occupying and living in the land of Canaan. If they decide to serve God, then they will realize the promises God made to Abraham, Isaac, and Jacob.

If they decide not to love God, then the curse awaits them. Their future hinges on this decision.

Although the decision to love God wholeheartedly initiates or opens the way of righteousness and the way of life, it can only be maintained by continual obedience.

Moses enjoins them to cleave unto God. This vital relationship with God requires exclusive devotion in daily life.

Paul, in speaking about salavtion in New Testament terms, makes use of this appeal made by Moses to the Israelites (cf. Deu 30:10-20 and Ro 10:1-21). Paul, like Moses, says that the message is plain and understandable. With the heart and mind, man responds to God—whether it is the Israelite in Moses' generation or the individual who listens to Paul's appeal. Faith and devotion Godward are essential. In Paul's time, however, the fuller revelation had been manifested in the person of Jesus Christ.

The alternative of choosing life or death was also emphasized in the teachings of Jesus. The one believing in Jesus Christ had the hope of eternal life, but the one who did not believe in Jesus was subject to the wrath of God (cf. Jn 3:1-36). Consequently, whether it is a matter of salvation through Christ or of the Israelite's relationship with God in the days of Moses, the choice man made when confronted with God's revelation had crucial and everlasting implications.

5

THE TRANSITION—MOSES TO JOSHUA

(31:1—34:12)

ALTHOUGH MAN'S TIME is limited, God's plan is continuous. Whereas man's abilities and opportunities are primarily related to a certain time and circumstance, God continues to operate through the changing times and successive generations to accomplish His plan and purpose. Moses was nearing the end of his responsibilities under God's appointment, and the time for replacement had come.

THE DIVINE ARRANGEMENT (31:1-29)

GOD'S APPOINTED LEADER (31:1-8)

Up to this point, Moses had been the key person in Israel. It was Moses who had responded to God's call to deliver the Israelites from the clutches of the Egyptian pharaoh. It was Moses who led the Israelites to Mount Sinai and there served as the mediator between God and the nation of Israel. It was through Moses that the greatest revelation of God to the Israelites occurred through the spoken word as well as in the mighty acts of God. Tirelessly, Moses had served during the last forty years of his life, having now reached the age of one hundred and twenty. The account of his activity and the content of that which God revealed through him to the Israelites as it is recorded in the books of Exodus, Leviticus, Numbers, and Deuteronomy constitute a greater part of the Old Testament than that which is given concerning any other individual in Old Testament times.

The life and ministry of Moses were now complete. God's directive was that Moses should not cross the Jordan River into the land of promise. This, however, did not affect God's plan and promise concerning the Israelites. Moses was not indispensable to the fulfillment of God's purpose. It was not the presence of Moses but rather the presence of God that was crucially important in the acquisition of the land of Canaan. Moses assures the Israelites that the presence and power of God will be manifested among the Israelites with Joshua as their leader. Joshua is coming to this position through God's appointment.

Since the Israelites will face fierce resistance in Canaan, Moses reminds them of the fact that God had recently given them victory over Sihon and Og, the kings of the Amorites. This recent manifestation of God's power on their behalf provided a reasonable basis for them to believe that God would give them similar victories in the future. Moses assures them that God will enable them to destroy these nations as God had commanded them previously through Moses. It was God who had done this under Moses—it is God who will do this under Joshua.

Moses assures them that God will do His part. Consequently, they are to be courageous and fearless. Boldly Moses asserts "for the LORD thy God, he it is that doth go with thee; he will not fail thee, nor forsake thee" (31:6b).

Having focused attention upon God's presence among them, Moses then presents Joshua to the Israelites as their leader. Publicly, Moses charges Joshua to go with the Israelites to possess the land God had sworn to the patriarchs. Joshua was the individual who was appointed by God to lead the Israelites in acquiring and possessing the land of promise.

Joshua is to set the example of being fearless and courageous. Moses does not leave him to his own resources but assures him personally as the future leader, "And the LORD, he it is that doth go before thee; he will be with thee, he will not fail thee, neither forsake thee: fear not, neither be dismayed" (31:8).

Whether it was Moses or Joshua as leader, the Israelites were to put their trust in God. The basic principle of accomplishing God's plan and purpose is the same today. Human leadership is important, but basically man's faith should be vested in God rather than man. It is God who actually enables and empowers. Leaders are expected to set the example of trusting in God so that together with the people, they recognize the necessity of divine enablement in accomplishing the tasks assigned.

GOD'S WRITTEN REVELATION (31:9-13)

What God had revealed through Moses to the Israelites was committed to writing. It was too crucial and vital to their future to be entrusted to memory and oral transmission. In the ancient Near East, matters that were important were not left to the care of bards or campfire romancers, but were carefully committed to a written form, so that future generations would have accurate knowledge. Certainly, that which was given by divine revelation was important enough to be preserved in written form.

"Moses wrote this law" does not necessarily mean that

Moses himself wrote the entire law in his own handwriting. Since Moses had seventy elders assisting him in handling the affairs of the Israelites it is very probable that he also had scribes writing for him. Very likely scribes recorded the speeches or addresses which Moses gave to the Israelites (Deu 1-30). In all likelihood, scribes assisted Moses in keeping an account of the journey in the wilderness, the details concerning the building of the tabernacle, the instructions concerning the sacrifices and the observance of the feasts and seasons, and the particular instructions concerning the ministry of the priests and Levites. Although assistants may have written much of this material preserved in the Pentateuch, it was Moses who was responsible for the final copies. They were written under his supervision and published under his name. Very likely these scribes who assisted Moses also wrote the account of Moses' death as given in Deuteronomy 34.

The priests and elders were given custody of the written copy of the law. The ark of the covenant was the holiest object in the camp of Israel. The priests had responsibility for the ark, which was associated with God's presence. The priests also had the responsibility of being guardians of the written law which expressly stated God's requirements. Consequently there could hardly have been a more appropriate place for safeguarding the written copy of the law than in close association with the ark of the covenant.

Together with the elders, the priests were responsible for reading the law publicly to the Israelites every seven years during the observance of the feast of tabernacles. In this way each generation would be exposed to the reading of the law from the written copy provided by Moses.

The purpose of the septennial reading of the law is explicitly stated. The Israelites were to learn to fear God by being exposed to the hearing of the law. Knowledge of the law or God's written revelation provided the basis for an intelligent response on the part of the hearers. Proper respect and reverence for God involved a conformity in their pattern of living in accordance with that which God had revealed to them.

The repetition of the public reading of the law every seven years provided each growing generation the opportunity to learn to fear and respect God. When parents and adults, as well as children, conformed to God's requirements in precept and example, then even those who did not understand the reading of the law had a God-fearing pattern of life imparted to them.

REVELATORY CONFIRMATION (31:14-23)

Joshua needed to be as certain that God had called him as Moses had been in his leadership responsibilities. Moses became aware of God's call when God spoke to him out of the burning bush. Repeatedly his call had been confirmed through miracles and the words spoken by God during the forty years of his ministry. Joshua had served as captain of the army when the Israelites defeated the Amalekites at Rephidim (Ex 17:9-14). He also had been one of the twelve spies sent into the land of Canaan from Kadesh-barnea to explore the promised land (Num 13:16). He and Caleb brought back a minority report encouraging the people to exercise faith in God to aid them in the conquest. When the people rebelled, Joshua and Caleb were the only two of that generation that were excluded from the judgment that fell upon all Israel. While the entire generation was doomed to die in the wilderness during the next four decades, Joshua and Caleb were assured that they would be privileged to enter the land promised to the patriarchs. This period of divine judgment had now run its full course.

Although God had spoken through Moses informing Joshua of his responsibilities as leader, God now brought to Joshua this confirmation through a supernatural manifestation that he was God's appointed man. Moses, reminded again that he must die, was divinely instructed to bring Joshua with him to the door of the tabernacle. There the pillar of cloud among them made both Moses and Joshua conscious of God's presence with them. This divine manifestation had first been evident at the Red Sea when the pillar of cloud provided divine protection for the escaping Israelites from the pursuing Egyptians (Ex 14-15). Throughout the wilderness journeys and encampments, this pillar of cloud had provided divine guidance and had hovered over the holiest part of the tabernacle where the ark of the covenant was located. Now God provided this divine revelatory confirmation at the entrance of the tabernacle as He spoke to Moses and Joshua.

God's message to Moses in Joshua's presence is summed up in 31:16-22. God, knowing the future, indicates that after Moses' death the Israelites will turn to idolatry. By forsaking God they will break their vital relationship with God. This breaking of the covenant will result in God's forsaking them. When God's presence is withdrawn and evil overtakes them, then the Israelites will wonder why such calamities have come upon them, until they recognize that their relationship with God has not been maintained.

God, being merciful, made provisions for such a time as this. Moses was instructed to write a song and teach it to the Israelites. The purpose of this song was explicitly stated. In written form it would be preserved and serve as a witness to the Israelites concerning that which God had done for them. Even though God will have forsaken them because they had forsaken Him, and His presence will have ceased to be evident among them, they will have available to them a written record of God's design and purpose. It is noteworthy that God did instruct Moses to provide a written copy for preservation so that it would be available to future generations.

To Joshua, God's message was direct and to the point of his commission. In the presence of Moses at the door of the tabernacle the divinely spoken word was,

1. Be strong and courageous.
2. You, Joshua, will bring the Israelites into Canaan, the land which I, God, had sworn to give to them.
3. I, God, will be with you.

This constituted the divine call and commission for Joshua to assume the leadership of Israel. With Moses being present, the continuity of Israel's leadership was divinely confirmed. Joshua was ordained and commissioned by God to succeed Moses as the leader of the Israelites.

THE DOCUMENTARY WITNESS (31:24-29)

The written copy of the law was to be kept with the ark of the covenant. Moses charged the Levites to care for this document as carefully as they did for the ark. The content of this written document was crucially important, for it communicated the essential principles so vital in their relationship with God.

Neither the ark nor the written copy of the law was to be worshiped. However, both were significantly important in their relationship with God. The written copy was to be available for reading, so that subsequent generations would have an accurate account of what God had done for them and an exact record of what God required of them as revealed through Moses. Moses knew human nature from his own experience. The Israelites had been rebellious while he was with them, and he knew that they would be rebellious and turn away from God after his death. In view of this prospect, Moses provided this written copy so that it would be a witness against them in their rebellion.

Requesting that the elders and officers be assembled, Moses addressed to them the words of this song (32:1-44), calling heaven and earth to witness against them. This song was written (31:19-22) and orally given by Moses to the assembly of Israelites before him.

THE DOCUMENT OF WITNESS (32:1-47)

This song of Moses is a remarkable speech made by Moses in poetic form. Since this ode was orally given to the generation of Israelites who were to enter Canaan and was written down for consideration by future generations who would live in Canaan, it reflects general conditions and attitudes rather than the limitations of Israel's experience in the past.

Moses was a prophet. Here he is speaking in terms of prophetic insight and understanding. Often he uses figurative language and does not make specific historic references as would be the case if this were prosaic history. In line with the true nature of prophecy, Moses makes statements that were characteristic of his contemporary generation as well as the generations to follow.

The benefits God bestowed upon Israel refer to the past from Moses' perspective and also characterize God's goodness to the Israelites in the future, as projected at various times by Moses as he speaks about the abundance of the land of promise. The references to the prosperity of the Israelites during later periods are not so specific as to warrant the viewpoint that this was written after the time of Moses. The Israelites under Moses had already experienced the greatest miracles and benefits of God's goodness by this time, and he was confident that God's mercy would continue toward them in the future. Moses assumes the future perspective when God's promises would have been fulfilled.

References to the oppression and exile are likewise in accord with what Moses had already stated would happen if the Israelites failed in their total commitment to God. Neither the Assyrians nor Chaldeans are specifically mentioned. Moses, however, from his own experience in Egypt was familiar with the nature of the conditions prevailing in times of slavery or oppression. In accordance with his predictions of Israel's behavior toward God, it was appropriate to portray the exilic conditions as the consequence of their disobedience. Nothing in this ode requires a post-Mosaic dating.

The general pattern of this ode is similar to suzerainty treaties of the Mosaic period. Recognizing this similarity Meredith Kline outlines this song of Moses as follows:

> Invocation, verses 1-3
> Suzerain identified, verses 4-6
> Historical prologue, verses 7-14
> Covenant broken, verses 15-18
> Consequence for Israel, verses 19-25
> Covenant renewal, verses 26-43[1]

INTRODUCTION (32:1-6)

Heaven and earth are summoned as witnesses of the covenant existing between God and the Israelites. Heaven and earth will verify Moses' public address to the people before him as he incorporates true wisdom and doctrine in his ascription of greatness to God.

The two parties in this relationship are specifically identified—God and the Israelites. God is described as "the Rock" or a reliable refuge for the Israelites (cf. 32:15, 18, 30). This God is absolutely righteous. He is faithful to His promise, true to His word, perfect in His work, just and right in His being.

The Israelites by contrast are corrupt in their dealings. By action they are no longer God's children but are crooked and perverse. Moses points out that they are foolish and senseless in repaying God who is their Father, creator, and sustainer, with such a corrupt pattern of living.

ISRAEL'S RECORD (32:7-18)

The historical perspective is clearly evident in the reference to past generations and elders. God had chosen the Israelites from among all nations. Abraham and his seed represented God's inheritance in this world. "Sons of Israel" (cf. KJV, ASV) is the reading of the traditional Hebrew text in verse eight; whereas in the Revised Standard Version and the New English Bible "sons of God" is based on several ancient versions and a Hebrew fragment from Qumran.

Providential love and care are bestowed upon Israel in the wilderness. Surrounded by wild beasts in a barren desert, Israel was tenderly cared for by God, who guarded them as a man would care for the apple of his eye or as an eagle cares for its young. In like manner, God also guided the Israelites through the desert to the land of Canaan. God provided the fruit of the field in abundance as well as the choicest of the flocks for the Israelites.

Although the Israelites enjoyed all these pleasures and benefits, they did not respond with gratitude but behaved like unruly beasts. "Jeshurun" seems to be used here sarcastically as a reference to Israel as "upright" or "righteous." In their arrogance the Israelites turned to idols, using what God had provided for them to make offerings to demons. Spurning God—the Rock of their salvation—in this manner, represented the height of ingratitude.

This type of apostasy and idolatry had already been witnessed by Moses during the period of his leadership. Knowing human nature, Moses even without prophetic insight could easily visualize what the idolatrous tendencies would be in future generations.

CONSEQUENCES OF ISRAEL'S ATTITUDE (32:19-25)

This breaking of their relationship with God precipitated divine judgment. The jealousy and wrath of a just and righteous God would be inescapable for the Israelites, who had spurned God's love and mercy and provoked God with their idolatry. They had been absorbed selfishly in the enjoyment of all the blessings God had so bountifully bestowed upon them. They had failed to express their gratitude toward God. Consequently, God would hide His face and withdraw His presence. Explicit was the prohibition concerning the worship and toleration of idols. A jealous God could not tolerate the recognition of idols, and consequently would abandon the unfaithful Israelites to famine, destruction, and conquest by their enemies.

Adultery was punishable by death. Israel in serving idols was adulterous in her relationship with God. Moses had already warned the Israelites that the curse of extinction threatened them if they should turn to the false gods in the land of Canaan (cf. 31:16-18). The terrors of pestilence, famine, and the sword awaited them (cf. Deu 28).

RESTORATION HOPES (32:26-43)

The judgment upon Israel would come for a redemptive purpose in the ultimate plan of God. The true servants of God would be avenged.

God's own glory is at stake in the complete destruction of Israel. If the enemy were successful in completely annihilating Israel, then the enemy would triumph and boast about his victory (32:26-27).

Foolish is the enemy that boasts about victory over God's chosen people. The enemy does not understand nor recognize that its victory over Israel has been made possible because Israel's Rock has sold His people and allowed them to be overpowered by the invader (32:28-30). Judgment came upon the Israelites under divine order because the moral corruption of the Israelites was like that of Sodom and Gomorrah's citizens (32:32-33). If God judged the Israelites who were His chosen people in this manner, how much greater would be God's judgment upon the enemies of Israel?

God will vindicate His people in vengeance upon the enemy. When the Israelites have been reduced to a complete bankruptcy and learned in their experience that the "no-gods" that they served could not help them (32:36-38), then God will avenge and recompense the enemy. The God of Israel will vindicate His people and once more show compassion for His servants (32:36, 39-42).

This song of Moses concludes with the prospect of jubilation and ultimate triumph (36:43). This appeal is to all nations to rejoice in the expiation of God's people and the execution of vengeance upon the adversaries of God. The enemies here are not necessarily the heathen nations, nor are the servants of God limited to God's chosen nation. Since this call to praise has a universal perspective, it represents the horizon of the Messianic age when all nations will experience the blessings promised to Abraham.

THE SONG'S CONCLUSION (32:44-47)

Significantly, Joshua was present when Moses proclaimed this song of witness (32:1-43), to the Israelites. Throughout the years of Moses' leadership, beginning with the defeat of the Amalekites at Rephidim (Ex 17), Joshua had been closely associated with Moses. What Moses expressed in this song about the Israelites and their tendencies toward idolatry was fully known to Joshua by way of experience and observation. Joshua had already been divinely commissioned in the special revelation at the entrance of the tabernacle (31:14-23).

The personal admonition to the Israelites was that they should fix their hearts on what God had revealed to them, so it would be significantly impressed upon their children. Exclusive devotion to and love for God is the key to life for the Israelites as a nation. Consequently, they should not consider this lightly nor secondary to any other matters. The way to enjoy life is to respond with a wholehearted commitment to God, reflected in their total pattern of living. The keeping of God's covenant was crucially important for them as well as for future generations.

MOSES THE MAN OF GOD (32:48—34:12)

The time for Moses' departure had come. His responsibilities of leadership were transferred to Joshua. Before he departs, Moses voices his blessing upon the Israelites and then ascends Mount Nebo to view the land of promise. There Moses died.

FINAL INSTRUCTIONS (32:48-52)

It must have been an impressive ceremony when Moses stood before the Israelites on his last day with them. The song of witness had been orally delivered with Joshua standing by his side. After Moses had given his final words of admonition to the people assembled before him, he received divine instructions. Very likely it was toward the close of that last day.

Moses was instructed to ascend Mount Nebo, which was one of the Abarim promontories of Moab, east of the Dead Sea and the Jordan River over against Jericho. He would be privileged to see the land of Canaan, to which entrance for him was not permitted.

Previously, Moses had been informed that he and Aaron would not be among those entering Canaan, because they had failed to exemplify an attitude of faith in God before the Israelites (Num 20:10-13; cf. Num 27:14; Deu 1:37; 3:26; 4:21). En route, Aaron died at Mount Hor (Num 20:22-29; 33:37-38; Deu 10:6). Before Moses departed to ascend Mount Nebo, he pronounced his blessing upon the Israelites whom he had served for four decades.

THE TESTAMENT OF MOSES (33:1-29)

Significance (33:1). The words of a dying father were very significant in ancient Near Eastern culture. A father's final words spoken to his sons were considered to be an irrevocable testament, acceptable as decisive evidence in court cases. The blessings given by the patriarchs to their sons (Gen 27:26-29; 39-40; 49:1-28), were recognized as crucially significant in their times. Beyond the legal recognition, the patriarchal blessings also had the supernatural aspect of the spirit of prophecy, whereby these men of God spoke what was divinely revealed to them.

In a sense Moses was the spiritual and theocratic father of the twelve tribes constituting the nation of Israel. Consequently this blessing which Moses pronounced upon the Israelites before his death can properly be called the testament of Moses. Joshua had already been designated as heir of the covenant in the sense that he was the dynastic successor of Moses. At the same time, all the Israelites were heirs of the covenant and thus recipients of God's blessings. The promises which were inheritable with the death of Moses became a reality when the testator died.

God revealed to Israel (33:2-5). The revelation of God through Moses constituted the most significant manifestation of God in Old Testament times. This was exceeded only by the fulness of God's revelation in the coming of Jesus Christ.

The description of the appearance of God as King is poetic (cf. other descriptions of this revelation of God in Judg 5:4-5; Ps 68:7-8, 17-18; Hab 3:2-6). Surrounded by "holy ones" from heaven, the presence of God was visible in the glory of the sunlike radiance over the mountains of Sinai. This manifestation of heavenly beings is also noted by the prophet Zechariah (14:5), by the psalmist (68:17), by Stephen (Ac 7:55-56), by Paul (Gal 3:19), and the author of the book of Hebrews (2:2).

The difficulty of describing the supernatural in any language is apparent in these verses. This is reflected in the problem of making accurate translations of this passage. What God and His heavenly host are like is beyond the ability of man to comprehend within the limitations of the human mind. The revelation at Mount Sinai represented a partial manifestation of God to the Israelites.

The giving of the law was a communication of God's will to the Israelites. God had chosen Israel as His people and now had made His love and mercy known to them in a majestic revelation.

With all the tribes gathered at Mount Sinai, God had made Himself known as their King. In Egypt they had been subjected to slavery under Pharaoh. Now they were to be "his righteous-nation" or Jeshurun. God's revelation to them at Mount Sinai was intended to provide them with sufficient knowledge of God's will, so that they were to live as a righteous nation and holy people identified with the King of kings (cf. Ex 19:4-6).

It was through Moses that this crucial revelation from God to man was made. Moses heard God speak, Moses received the written copies of the law, Moses represented the Israelites in receiving the law, and Moses made intercession for the Israelites when they precipitated God's wrath. Moses was the key man between God and man in the greatest revelation in Old Testament times.

The tribal blessings (33:6-25). Moses expresses his blessings for the tribes of Israel in the forms of doxologies, prayers, predictions, and imperatives. His familiarity with each of the tribes and his knowledge of the words of Jacob (Gen 49), are reflected at various times.

The order in which the sons of Jacob are blessed is as follows; the sons of Leah, the sons of Rachel, and then the sons of their handmaids.

For the Reubenites, Moses prayed a prayer of survival. Although Reuben was the oldest, Jacob withheld from him the blessing of the firstborn. Apparently Reuben had never asserted the right of the firstborn. When Joseph was sold by his brethren, Reuben did not exert enough influence to prevent his enslavement.

Judah, Leah's fourth son, had been singled out by Jacob as bearing the scepter. Moses prays that Judah may emerge among his people as victor over their enemies.

Although Simeon *and* Levi had been rebuked by Jacob (Gen 49:5-7), Moses omits Simeon and prays that the Levites might be singularly blessed by God as they are distributed throughout the rest of the tribes. The Simeonites received a number of cities in the southern territory of Judah (Jos 19:2-9), and did not lose their identity. Thirteen Simeonite princes are noted in the days of Hezekiah (1 Ch 4:34-38). The Levites, however, are designated as the priestly tribe among the Israelites. At Mount Sinai at the crucial time of Israel's idol worship, the Levites distinguished themselves for their devotion to God (Ex 32:26-29).

Being allotted forty-eight cities throughout the tribes of Israel, the Levites were charged with special responsibilities under the supervision of the priesthood of the Aaronic family. The Urim and Thummim, worn by the high priest, represented God's pledge that His will would be made known among the Israelites (Ex 28:29-30). In addition to receiving divine revelation, the priests were also responsible for teaching the law and officiating at the sacrifices. In this ministry the Levites were to assist the priests.

Moses next speaks of the sons of Rachel. The tribe of Benjamin is assured a safe dwelling place. It was allotted the land northward of Judah near Jerusalem. Joseph, the oldest son of Rachel, was given the double portion in that both Ephraim and Manasseh as the sons of Joseph enjoyed tribal status. As Jacob had done before him, Moses indicated that Ephraim would have the preeminence over Manasseh. Ephraim emerged as the foremost tribe in the Northern Kingdom after the partition of Solomon's empire. The tribes of Joseph are endowed with military power, even as Jacob had indicated.

Zebulun and Issachar, the sixth and fifth sons of Leah respectively, were to be blessed with the wealth of the sea, apparently secured by trade. Moses expresses the hope that this success in material things will result in their concern to offer to God the right sacrifices.

The doxology concerning Gad indicates that the Gadites received the initial portion of the conquered land east of the Jordan River. They had already promised that they would participate in the conquest of the rest of Palestine, even though they already had secured their allotment east of the Jordan River.

Dan is compared to the lions of Bashan, as far as his energy is concerned. Jacob had compared him to a serpent

(Gen 49:17-19). Naphtali is assured of the Lord's favor and blessing. For the people of Asher, Moses prayed that they might enjoy prosperity and strength.

God and Israel (33:26-29). As Moses concludes the blessings for his people, he reflects once more on the majesty and greatness of God, and how fortunate Israel is to be identified with this God.

God is without equal. The heavens provide the course for His path in coming to aid the Israelites. In majestic greatness God traversed the skies. In space God is unlimited and in time God cannot be contained—He is eternal and everlasting. It is this God whose everlasting arms uphold and sustain Israel. It is this God who is the dwelling place for Israel.

Moses identifies Israel as Jeshurun, "the upright." In spite of his personal knowledge concerning the sinful tendencies and ways of the Israelites he thinks of them as "the upright" ones. This undoubtedly reflected his prayer, wishes, and hopes for them in their future relationship with God.

With God serving as Israel's dwelling place and His presence permeating the land of Canaan, the enemy would be destroyed, and Israel would dwell in safety. Moses envisioned the Israelites enjoying the bounteous fruits of Canaan enriched by the dew of heaven.

The Israelites, having a God who is unequaled and so concerned with Israel, are unique among the nations of the world. There is no nation to be compared with them. Israel is a nation above all nations. All other nations will eventually be subservient to God's chosen people.

GOD'S APPOINTED SUCCESSION (34:1-12)

This account provides a fitting conclusion to the book of Deuteronomy as well as to the Pentateuch. Insofar as

God's covenant with Israel involved Moses, it was necessary for Moses to die before Joshua could become the servant who represented God as the leader of Israel.

Moses' death and burial (34:1-8). With the conclusion of this blessing, Moses departed from Israel to walk alone up Mount Nebo to the top of Pisgah. Mount Nebo reaches an altitude of 2,740 feet at a point twelve miles east of the entrance of the Jordan River into the Dead Sea, 1,292 feet below sea level. From this vantage point Moses was permitted to see the land of promise.

Looking to the north, Moses could see the Jordan valley extending beyond the Sea of Galilee to the snowcapped peak of Mount Hermon—120 miles to the north, where it formed the southern terminus of the Anti-Lebanon range, 9,232 feet above sea level. Although the Mediterranean Sea may not have been visible to Moses, he viewed the land directly westward before him, especially the lush oasis surrounding Jericho, which the Israelites anticipated as their possession as soon as they crossed the Jordan River. In this manner Moses viewed the land which God had promised to Abraham, Issac, and Jacob.

On Mount Nebo, Moses the servant of the Lord died. He was buried in the Moabite valley but the exact place of his burial is unknown (cf. Jude 9). Moses did not die of old age, even though he was an hundred and twenty years old. Neither his eyesight nor his vigor (life-force, a rare word found elsewhere only in Ugaritic from before 1200 B.C.) had diminished. His mission as God's servant had been fulfilled. His life expired at the command of God. The Israelites mourned his death for thirty days.

Ordained succession (34:9-12). Moses as the servant of God and in accordance with the command of God had ordained Joshua as his successor by the laying on of hands.

The charismatic gifts of wisdom were bestowed on Joshua. The Israelites acknowledged Joshua as their divinely ordained leader.

Moses was unique among the prophets in Israel. In this divine-human relationship, God knew Moses "face to face." No human being had had as much communicated to him by divine revelation as Moses had imparted to him as God's spokesman. The greatest miracle of all Old Testament times was the deliverance of the Israelites from Egyptian bondage. In divine revelation through word as well as the mighty acts of God displayed through his ministry, Moses was never equaled by any subsequent prophet until the coming of Jesus Christ.

Although no memorial marker was erected to identify the tomb of Moses, he was not forgotten. The revelation as recorded in the Pentateuch was remembered as the law of Moses from generation to generation. Prophet after prophet reminded the Israelites that God had spoken through Moses. So did Jesus. Moses next appears in history on the mount of transfiguration together with the prophet Elijah and the Lord Jesus Christ (Mt 17:3; Mk 9:4; Lk 9:30-31).

NOTES

INTRODUCTION

1. Julius Wellhausen, *Prolegomena to the History of Israel* (Edinburgh, 3rd-ed. 1885), p. 9.
2. For a recent statement of this viewpoint, see E. W. Nicholson, *Deuteronomy and Tradition* (Philadelphia: Fortress, 1967); cf. G. E. Wright, "Deuteronomy," *Interpreter's Bible* 2(1953), and more recently, an excellent summary of this hypothesis by Gerald A. Larue in *Old Testament Life and Literature* (Boston: Allyn & Bacon, 1968), pp. 26-39.
3. For a representative discussion of this viewpoint of Mosaic authorship, see R. K. Harrison, *Introduction to the Old Testament* (Grand Rapids: Eerdmans, 1969), pp. 635-62; cf. E. J. Young, *Introduction to the Old Testament* (Grand Rapids: Eerdmans, 1963), pp. 99-112; and G. L. Archer, *A Survey of Old Testament Introduction* (Chicago: Moody, 1964), pp. 239-50.
4. Cf. Meredith Kline, *Treaty of the Great King* (Grand Rapids: Eerdmans, 1963), p. 28. As a covenant renewal document, the book of Deuteronomy can be outlined as follows:
   a. Preamble (1:1-5)
   b. Historical prologue (1:6—4:49)
   c. Stipulations (5:1—26:19)
   d. Curses and blessings (27:1—30:20)
   e. Arrangements for succession and public reading (31:1—34:12)

1.

1. Kline, pp. 47-49. The parallel structure between God's covenant with Israel and the suzerainty or vassal type of international treaty found in the Near East during the Mosaic age is significant. The book of Deuteronomy claims to represent the farewell and ceremonial addresses of Moses in which he renews the covenant to the second generation of Israelites. As God's servant people, the Israelites were to commit themselves to obey Joshua who represented God's reign symbolically in the earthly mediatorial dynasty. From

the standpoint of literary structure, Kline identifies the essential parts of ancient treaties in Deuteronomy. (See Introduction, n. 4, this volume.)

5.

1. Kline, "Deuteronomy," *The Wycliffe Bible Commentary* (Chicago: Moody, 1962), pp. 199-200. See also Kline, *Treaty of the Great King,* pp. 138-44.

BIBLIOGRAPHY

COMMENTARIES AND DEVOTIONAL BOOKS

Barclay, Robert A., *The Lawgivers: Leviticus and Deuteronomy.* London: Lutterworth, 1964.

Blair, Edward P. "The Book of Deuteronomy." In *The Layman's Bible Commentary.* Richmond, Va.: Knox, 1964.

Cunliffe-Jones, H. "Deuteronomy." In *Torch Bible Commentaries.* London: S. C. M. Press, 1951.

Driver, S. R. "Deuteronomy." In *International Critical Commentary.* New York: Scribner, New York, 1895.

Francisco, Clyde G. *The Book of Deuteronomy.* Grand Rapids: Baker, 1964.

Hanke, Howard A. "Numbers and Deuteronomy." In *The Weslyan Bible Commentary,* edited by C. Carter. Grand Rapids: Eerdmans, 1967.

Harrison, R. K. "Deuteronomy." In *The New Bible Commentary Revised,* ed. D. Guthrie and J. A. Motyer. Grand Rapids: Eerdmans, 1970.

Keil, C. F., and Delitzsch, F. *Pentateuch: Biblical Commentary on the Old Testament.* Vol. 3. Translated by J. Martin. Grand Rapids: Eerdmans, 1949.

Kline, Meredith. "Deuteronomy." In *The Wycliffe Bible Commentary,* edited by C. H. Pfeiffer and E. H. Harrison. Chicago: Moody, 1962.

——— . *Treaty of the Great King.* Grand Rapids: Eerdmans, 1963.

Manley, G. T. *The Book of the Law.* London: Tyndale House, 1957.

McCarthy, D. J. *Treaty and Covenant.* Rome: Pontifical Bib. Inst., 1963.

Reider, J. *Deuteronomy.* Philadelphia: Jewish Pub. Soc., 1939.

Schultz, S. J. *The Prophets Speak.* New York: Harper & Row, 1968.

Sully, Linda L. "The Love of God for Israel." Thesis, Wheaton Col., Ill., 1968.

Von Rad, Gerhard. *Studies in Deuteronomy.* London: S. C. M. Press, 1953.

Wright, G. E. "The Book of Deuteronomy." In *The Interpreter's Bible,* vol. 2. Nashville: Abingdon, 1953.

AUTHORSHIP AND INTRODUCTION

Archer, Gleason L. *A Survey of Old Testament Introduction.* Chicago: Moody, 1964.

Gottwald, N. A. *A Light to the Nations.* New York: Harper & Row, 1959.

Harrison, R. K. *Introduction to the Old Testament.* Grand Rapids: Eerdmans, 1969.

Kitchen, Kenneth A. *Ancient Orient and Old Testament.* Chicago: Inter-Varsity, 1966.

Nicholson, E. W. *Deuteronomy and Tradition.* Philadelphia: Fortress, 1967.

Pfeiffer, R. H. *Introduction to the Old Testament.* New York: Harper & Brothers, 1941.

Schultz, Samuel J. *The Old Testament Speaks.* 2d ed. New York: Harper & Brothers, 1970.

Young, E. J. *An Introduction to the Old Testament.* Grand Rapids: Eerdmans, 1949.